Western
Edible
Wild
Plants

by H.D. HARRINGTON

Illustrated by Y. MATSUMURA

THE UNIVERSITY OF NEW MEXICO PRESS

TABLE OF CONTENTS

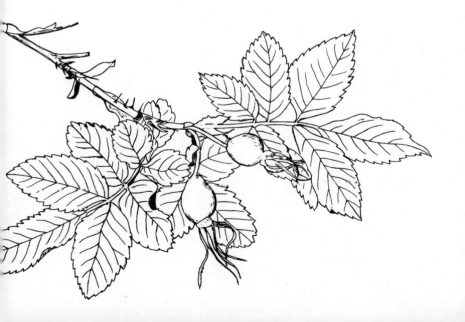

INTRODUCTION

THE STUDY of edible native plants has been of interest and concern to many people in the past; in fact such knowledge has sometimes been a matter of survival itself. Recently there has been a revival of this interest and a number of books and articles have appeared dealing with edible plants, usually treating those of a limited area. This book covers the plants growing in an area bounded on the east by western Nebraska and Kansas, on the west by the Pacific Ocean and stretches south to include New Mexico, Arizona and southern California, north to the Black Hills of South Dakota and the state of Washington. This area is referred to here as the "West." We have tried to write for botanists and nonbotanists alike. The plant descriptions are in nontechnical language, but we have tried to make them strictly accurate. The botanical names are given for those who may want them but may be ignored by the nonbotanists. These scientific names are the ones used in the various treatments covering the western flora. We have listed all the common names for each species that we have heard used in this area, but the reader may know the plant by one that we have never encountered. There is no law in the use of such names as we find in the case of botanical ones. This is discussed at some length in Chapter III of Harrington's *How to Identify Plants*. It follows that your own common names are just as "legal" as the ones used here.

We have selected for the drawings representative and widely distributed species of the group. The illustrations include not only a sketch of the mature plant in flower or fruit but also enlargements of those special parts that botanists consider to be diagnostic. This will allow the reader to become acquainted with the plant in the only stage when it can be identified with real accuracy, that is in flower and fruit. An absolutely correct determination is of prime importance. We suggest that when checking the drawings you refer to the *"Key to Abbreviations"* at the back of this introduction, particularly if you have had some botanical training.

The information contained in this book was assembled in several different ways:

1. Actual personal experiments of the author extending throughout many years.

2. Information from numerous courageous collaborators. Among these investigators were Professor Y. Matsumura (the illustrator), Edith Harrington, Dr. N. Oshima, Dr. Mary Meserve, Dr. Robert Irving, Professor Bruno Klinger, Dr. John Douglass, Margaret Douglass, Professor Benjamin Gardner, Owen Smith, Angello Cuzetto, William Sears, Marilyn Colyer, Dr. Jack May, Dr. Charles Bagdonas and Maurine Frederick. They all remained in good health throughout the experiments!

3. Specific information contributed by many interested people, this help acknowledged throughout the text in the appropriate place.

4. Information on the subject of useful wild plants found in various books and articles. Our own list of those consulted now runs well over 600 items. If you want to check 259 of them, especially when the author or authors are mentioned here specifically, they are listed at the back of the author's book *Edible Native Plants of the Rocky Mountains*. When we formally started this project in 1960, our colleague, Professor Claire Norton, and in addition Dr. Edward Castetter, who was formerly at the University of New Mexico, very generously turned over to us their extensive bibliographies on useful native plants. Among these items were many on the subject of

ethnobotany, which deals with the use of plants by the Indians of the region. This aspect of the matter is important in a study of this kind since the Indians in the past had learned to use many species of plants, particularly in times of extreme food shortage. Because of the change in lifeways of the modern Indians, much of this detailed knowledge may well be lost entirely unless someone puts it on record. The same thing can be said for the information on edible native plants once known to the white pioneers of the area. Some of this knowledge has been passed on to their descendants; much of it either has been or will be forgotten.

Some native plants are palatable and nutritious; unfortunately, others are bad tasting or actually may be poisonous. It follows that those people who wish to eat such food should know the species involved, just as they recognize the ones in their gardens. After all, when you go out to gather a mess of lettuce, you don't mistake it for ragweed that may be growing nearby. If you do you are certainly in for a surprisingly new taste sensation! The very best way to learn plants is to develop the ability to identify them in the technical floras and manuals covering the region. This skill is rather difficult to acquire, especially outside of a formal course, and few of us have the opportunity, the time, or the energy to master it. The author's *How to Identify Plants* does provide practical help in this respect. If you want to dine on native plants and do not wish to formally develop the technique of keying them out, then we suggest the following:

1. Fix in mind the appearance of some edible plant you already know (like *Typha*—ordinary cattail). Watch it throughout the growing season, from the time it pushes its shoots above the ground until it develops flowers and fruits. You may want to utilize it at various stages of its growth, even in winter, so you must be able to recognize it at any time. About 2000 years ago a famous herbalist, Dioscorides pointed this out by re-

minding us: "Now it behooves anyone who desires to be a skillful herbalist, to be present when the plants first shoot out of the earth, when they are fully grown, and when they begin to fade." This initial acquaintance can be gained by having an edible plant pointed out to you by some knowledgeable friend. Also, you can often identify it yourself by comparing it carefully with a drawing, photograph, or description, such as one of those given in this book. When you have learned one plant in all its growth phases, you are ready to start in on others. Before long, you will have built up quite a list of plants you know are good to eat. In any case, our advice is to go easy on each new trial and consume a small to moderate amount at first. It is possible that you may have actually misidentified the plant and trustfully tackled a harmful one. Then again, perhaps you may have some special allergic reaction to some species that is harmless to most people. But once you are sure the plant is healthful for you, then you may proceed without fear. There is seldom a lack of such material in nature.

2. Better learn the common poisonous plants of the area, particularly those that are likely to be mistaken for edible ones. For example, if you want to eat the bulbs of wild onion (*Allium*), then you should know not only exactly what these onions look like but you should also be able to recognize death camas (*Zigadenus*), which also bears bulbs and is apt to grow nearby. Stockmen, government agencies, county agricultural agents, etc., can help you learn these poisonous plants. You can also get some assistance from various books and state bulletins, which list and often provide drawings of such species. A few of our own common poisonous plants are illustrated and described in the final chapter.

When you wish to test out a likely looking edible species, in times of emergency for example, then the following rules are worth remembering:

1. Place a small portion of the raw plant in your mouth; chew,

but do not swallow. Then remove it and wait for unfavorable reactions such as a burning, stinging or numbing sensation.

2. If all is well, chew up and swallow a small piece of the raw plant. Wait for at least an hour before you proceed.

3. Then cook some of the plant and swallow a small portion. If serious ill effects develop, induce vomiting.

4. Wait several hours, then eat a small to moderate amount of the raw or cooked portion. Do this several times over an interval of several hours.

5. If all goes well up to this point, it is safe to eat this new food in reasonable quantities.

6. If you have a limited amount of familiar food along, we suggest that you gradually work in the new food with the old. In any event, we advise that you do not gorge yourself on the unfamiliar food, at least for a time. Surely when you are under survival conditions is not the time to risk becoming physically sick!

If the above rules are followed, then there is no reason for anyone to endure extreme hunger in any place in the West, even in the winter time. The inner bark of many trees can be peeled off and eaten raw or cooked. The algae and aquatic plants of rivers, ponds, and lakes can also be used to sustain life. Some people have claimed that even the silt or mud at the bottom of ponds and lakes can be cooked into a souplike mixture. Herter has stated that Robert Beauchamp, Director of the East African Fisheries Research Organization, once fed himself and his family for a time on the mud from the bottom of Lake Victoria. This all seems a bit extreme; certainly more palatable sounding food is usually available if one knows where to look for it. In any event a number of experienced outdoor people have stated flatly, "If you starve to death in the wilderness, it is because you are just plain tired of living." This is probably an overstatement for the sake of emphasis, but it is true that the food is there, and it is certainly your own fault if you don't utilize it.

The widespread practice that individuals or agencies have of spraying plants with various insecticides or weedicides (herbicides) has created a minor problem for anyone wishing to utilize edible native plants. Much of these chemical deposits can be removed by washing the plant parts thoroughly, and even those that are actually absorbed into the plant body are usually very low in toxicity in the amounts ordinarily present. However, we would not care to eat these sprayed plants ourselves, and advise you to secure your edible plant material well away from these treated areas. Such sprayed patches are usually in or around fields of cultivated crop plants, or along roadsides.

We wish to acknowledge the financial support of the United States Department of Health, Education and Welfare during the period from 1960 to 1963, support that allowed us to travel over the region in order to collect and try out many of the plants mentioned in this book.

We now have records of many more food plants than are mentioned here; we may have left out some of your favorite ones. We know just how you may feel about it because lack of space forced us to also omit many of our own!

General Key to Abreviations of Drawings

A—Annulus of Fungus
Ac—*Allium cernuum*
Ag—*Allium geyeri*
Aw—Awn
B—Bulb (or bulblike corm)
BL—Basal Leaf
Br—Bract
C—Calyx of Flower
CFr—Cross-section Fruit
Cl—*Claytonia lanceolata*
Cm—*Claytonia megarrhiza*
Cg—*Calochortus gunnisonii*
Cn—*Calochortus nuttallii*
F—Flower
FC—Fruit Cluster
FH—Fruit Head
Fr—Fruit
FSp—Fruit Spike
G—Gill of Fungus
H—Habit of Plant
In—Inflorescence
L—Leaf
Li—Ligule of Leaf

Nb—New Bud
O—Ovary of Flower
P—Perianth Part
Pa—Petal of Flower
Pb—*Polygonum bistortoides*
Pi—Pistil of Flower
Pv—*Polygonum viviparum*
R—Root
Rh—Rhizome
Rs—Rootstock
S—Seed
Sn—Stamen of Flower
Sp—Spike
Spl—Spikelet
Tr—Taproot
UL—Upper Leaf
V—Volva Cup of Fungus
X—Times enlarged (x2 = twice natural size on original drawing)
♀ —Female or Pistillate
♂ —Male or Staminate

CHAPTER I: UNDERGROUND PARTS
(like Radish or Carrot)

THESE BELOW-GROUND STRUCTURES are very useful as sources of food in many native plants. For one thing, they are available the year round if one knows where and how to locate them. In fact, many such roots and underground parts are at their very best in the fall or winter. However, using them poses a problem as to the correct identification of the plant, since the plant stems at that season may have withered, the flowers will have disappeared and only the old parts of the plants remain above ground. The root parts often look much alike on different species, and the possibility always exists that material from harmful plants may have been gathered by mistake. Even Indians seemed to have been sometimes guilty of this error. This becomes of particular importance when one notes that poisonous substances, when present, are often concentrated in the underground parts of the plant. Of course, if they are gathered in the spring or summer when flowers are present (to aid in recognition), this special problem is not so acute. *Do not use the underground parts of any plant unless you are sure of the species involved.*

Another advantage is that root parts often provide comparatively large amounts of reasonably nutritious food. Also, they can be stored for a reasonable length of time, and can be carried from areas where they are readily available to other parts of the country. This may be of special value in food-emergency situations. Of course, they are rather heavy but they can be easily sliced, dried in the sun, then be readily transported. Such dehydrated root parts keep for months or even years according to our experiences; when soaked again in water, they cook into a palatable food.

The term "underground parts" is used here to include any thickened structure borne by the plant below the ground level. Such structures as true roots, rhizomes (cattail), tubers (potatoes), corms (crocus) and bulbs (onions) are included in this general concept. By utilizing these edible underground parts, the Indians and the early pioneers were able to survive during many periods of serious food shortage, especially when these occurred in the winter time.

Typha spp.
CATTAIL

Description:

Perennial plants with thick underground rootstocks; stems 2½ to as much as 8 feet tall; leaves long and narrow, up to 1 inch wide; spikes variable in length but the lower seed-bearing hairy portion 2 to 12 inches long, some shade of brown at maturity, the pollen-bearing upper portion about as long; fruits very small, seed-like, bearing hairs, very many crowded together.

In marshes, shallow lakes, ditches and stream borders in moister wet places. The species are very widely distributed in Eurasia and North America. Scattered over the West, usually below 8,000 feet.

Use:

This is probably the most famous of all the edible plants of the Northern Hemisphere. It has been called "an outdoor pantry." The Boy Scouts of this area have a saying, "You name it, we'll make it with cattails." Certainly no one should starve

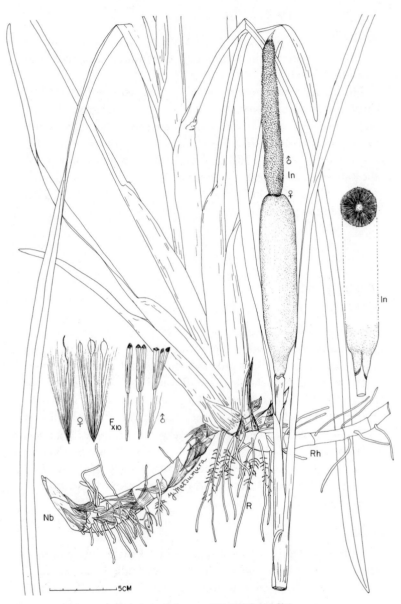

COMMON CATTAIL (*Typha latifolia*)

or even go hungry in an area where cattails are abundant. They were favorite plants with the Indians, who used them as food throughout most of the year. The young shoots were pulled or cut from the rootstocks in the spring when they were about 4 to 16 inches long. The outer leaves were peeled away, leaving the tender golden-yellow inner portion; these were eaten raw or in salads. We found them delicious when chopped with lettuce, tomatoes and cucumbers. These young shoots can be used as a potherb, as they are in Russia, where they are called "Cossack asparagus," or they can be cooked in other various ways, even made into a kind of soup. Even when the shoots are 1 to 2 feet long they can still be utilized. These young shoots are more prevalent in the springtime, but do appear throughout the summer and fall. Try boiling them for 25-35 minutes, serving them with butter and seasoning. We consider them excellent in flavor.

As the season progresses the young flower stalks begin to appear. These spikes can be taken out of their sheaths and cooked in various ways. When boiled for 20 minutes you can eat them like roasting ears, nibbling the flowers off the tough inner stalk. The flowers, especially the pollen-producing ones on the upper part, can be scraped off and used alone, or as flavoring or thickening for other foods.

When the plants have further ripened, but the pollen has not been shed, we have sometimes stripped off these pollen-producings flowers by hand, often gathering several pounds in an hour or two. These young flowers can be used to make muffins, cookies, biscuits or pancakes, when mixed with wheat flour in equal proportions. They can be preserved for future use by spreading them out on a flat pan. Put this in a preheated oven set at about 350 degrees F. and roast the flowers until they are perfectly dry, stirring them frequently to avoid burning. They can then be stored for long periods in a dry, closed container, and can eventually be used in the same way as the fresh ones.

After the pollen starts to be shed naturally, it can be collected by shaking the flowers in a container. A surprising amount of this yellow dust can often be collected in a reasonable amount of time. If this pollen is shaken in the can, the chaff and insects will rise to the top and can be removed. This pollen, when mixed with flour, can be used like the flowers for making muffins, cookies, biscuits, cakes or pancakes. Pancakes made with cattail pollen are famous. Try the following recipe.

Mrs. Norton's Cattail Flapjacks

2 cups cattail pollen (or flowers) ½ cup evaporated milk
2 cups wheat flour   1½ cups water
4 teaspoons baking powder   1 tablespoon syrup
1 teaspoon salt   bacon drippings
2 eggs

Beat eggs, add milk, water and syrup. Mix and add dry ingredients, beating until mixture is creamy. Add bacon drippings. Fry in a hot greased pan over the camp fire. Makes about 20 cakes.

After the tops of the cattails have turned brown in the fall the rootstocks are a source of food. In fact, they are available at any time, but seem to us to be richer in starch at the end of the growing season. They are usually found about 3-4 inches below the soil surface. We like the young rootstocks best; these are the ones that have a bud at the end ready to form the new growth in the spring. The outer peel should be removed and the central white core, often ⅜ to ½ inch in diameter, will be found to make up about 50% to 60% of the rootstock. These cores can be eaten raw; they have a pleasant starchy taste, but contain harsh fibers that interfere somewhat with the enjoyment of eating them; we think they are better boiled or baked.

Cattail rootstocks are fairly high in starch content; this is usually listed at about 30% to 46%. This can be extracted to form a flour which compares favorably with that from wheat, corn and rice in percentages of fats, proteins and carbohydrates. The flour can be secured in at least two ways. The rootstock cores can be dried, then pounded in a metate or ground up in a grinder. The fibers can then be sifted out and the flour secured. Water can be used in the process since the flour will readily settle to the bottom; then the liquid is poured off. Another method suggested by Gibbons is to fill a large container with cold water then shred, manipulate and crush the cores with the hands in the water until the fibers are separated and washed clean. Then strain out these fibers and allow the flour to settle for about 30 minutes. The water can then be poured off and fresh water added again. After another half hour pour off the water again. The flour will still have enough moisture so that it can be worked like dough.

The buds at the end of the young rootstocks have a lump of starchy material in their centers where they join the main rootstock; this starchy mass is also present after the buds develop into young shoots; it is greatly fancied by many people. Cattail flour is a potential source of food for the population since this plant covers many thousand acres in the United States. Classen figured that one acre of cattails would yield about 6,475 pounds of flour. This flour would probably contain about 80% carbohydrates and around 6% to 8% protein. It does appear that this is a potential source of food, produced by land not suitable for growing most other crop plants. Harvesting the rootstock cores would be a problem and we do not expect the production of cattail flour to become a major industry. As a source of emergency food these rootstocks are ideal.

The Indians would sometimes eat the tiny seedlike fruits, by burning off the bristles. This process would roast or parch the "seeds," which could then be rubbed off the spike. Sometimes the down was pulled off the spike and spread on a flat rock. This

was burned and the minute "seeds" swept up to be used as food.
Finally, the cattail down was sometimes stripped off the spikes
and used to provide padding in pillows, blankets and for the
Indian cradle board. Certainly, there is no more useful edible
native plant than the cattail.

Species:

Narrow-leaf cattail (*T. angustifolia*) and common cattail (*T. latifolia*) are widely distributed throughout North America.
The species illustrated, *T. latifolia,* is usually more abundant
and the edible parts are larger. Two others may be present but
resemble the one figured both in appearance and use.

Nuphar spp. (*Nymphaea*)
COWLILY, POND LILY, SPATTERDOCK, YELLOW WATERLILY

Description:

Plants from thick rootstocks which are anchored in the soil
at the bottom of rather shallow water of lakes and ponds; leaf
blades large, up to 16 inches long, usually on long stalks that
let them float on the surface, but sometimes actually raise them
in the air; flowers large, the petals or segments up to 1¼ inches
long, yellow but often tinged with red or fading whitish; fruit
up to hen's-egg size, becoming leathery and podlike, containing
many large seeds.

Growing in lakes, ponds, or slow streams. Scattered pretty
well throughout North America, in the West most common in
high mountain lakes of the northern and middle parts.

Use:

Cowlily rootstocks are buried in the mud, often in water 4 to
5 feet deep. The Indians would often dive for them and would

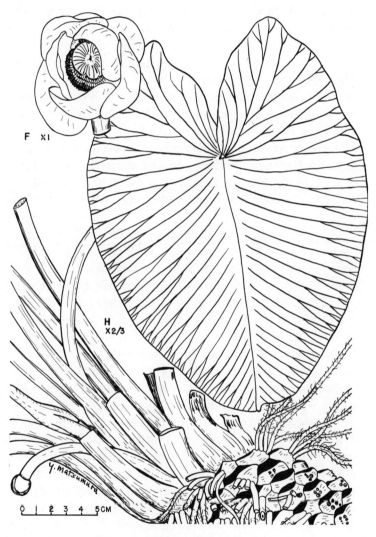

F x1

H
x2/3

y. Matsumura

0 1 2 3 4 5CM

COWLILY (*Nuphar polysepalum*)

bring up chunks as much as 2 feet long. These were usually boiled or baked. The rind was then removed and the spongy, glutinous, slightly sweet contents were used in various ways, often with meat. The Air Force Manual suggested peeling the fresh rootstocks, cutting the centers into thin slices and allowing them to dry. These slices can then be ground or pulverized. Then the meal can be soaked in water, the water poured off carefully, and this repeated several times; this is said to remove the strong taste. The meal or flour can then be dried and used in various ways, such as making gruel or in thickening soup. These rootstocks are sometimes stored in muskrat houses, which cache the Indians often raided. In time of emergency this could be done by anyone. They are usually collected in the fall, but would be available at any season when the water was not frozen solid.

The fruit pods contain numerous seeds which have been used in various ways. For example, try drying the large pods and pounding out the hard seeds which can then be further dried in the sun. The pods can also be broken open in a pan of water and the seeds separated from the sticky pulp by washing, then dried in the sun. These seeds can be stored for winter use to be processed when needed. In any case, when you need them you can parch the seeds in a frying pan over a slow fire, stirring the seeds as you would do in popping corn. They may pop open slightly, somewhat like unenthusiastic popcorn. These parched seeds are pounded or lightly ground and the hard shells removed by winnowing, shaking or by picking them out with the fingers. The kernels can be ground up to make a meal, or after additional parching can be eaten like peanuts. The meal can be used in various ways. Norton suggested using 2 cups of boiling water, stirring in 1 cup of the meal. Boil for 15 minutes stirring constantly and then simmering it with very low heat for an hour. This can be eaten hot like mush or cooled, sliced and fried in butter.

The various species of cowlily formed one of the important foods to the early Indians, especially in the Northwest. It can be an emergency food of no small importance, and the rhizomes or seeds may be available in just the places where food may be desperately needed.

Species:

The common species of the West is *N. polysepalum* (the one figured) with *N. variegatum* coming into the area from western Canada. *N. advena* of the eastern United States is used like our species.

Calochortus spp.
MARIPOSA LILY, SEGO LILY, SEGOLILY MARIPOSA

Description:

Plants growing from deep-set, thick-scaled bulbs, often with additional bulblike swellings on the stems about at ground level; stems usually rather erect, unbranched except near the top, often to over a foot tall; leaves narrow and grasslike; flowers large and showy often up to 3 inches wide, whitish, cream-colored, yellow, purplish, pinkish, orange to nearly scarlet, the petals about as broad as long; fruit a narrow dry pod (capsule) with 3 compartments within.

Throughout the West. Open slopes, plains and meadows or in partial shade growing from low elevations nearly up to timberline.

Use:

These were important food plants to the Indians and the early pioneers. In fact, they are credited with saving the lives of many Mormon settlers, especially during the fall of 1848 when

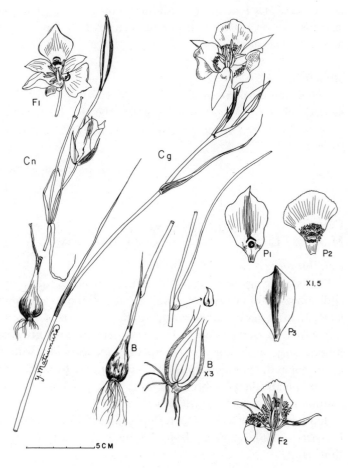

MARIPOSA LILY (*Calochortus gunnisonii & C. nuttallii*)

the crops were damaged by a horde of crickets. In gratitude, one of the species (*C. nuttallii*), was made the state flower of Utah under the name sego lily. Incidentally, a statue in honor of the sea gulls that helped destroy the crickets, stands on the temple grounds in Salt Lake City.

The whole plant is edible and has been used as a potherb, but is hardly bulky enough to provide much material. The seeds have been ground as food and the flower buds have been eaten raw as a kind of salad. However, it is the thick-scaled bulbs that are the real delicacy and the source of a good food supply. These bulbs are rather small (rarely over 1 inch in diameter), and are borne about 5 or 6 inches underground. They break off readily from the stem and may be easily overlooked in the ground. It is not an easy matter to secure an adequate amount but it is certainly worth the effort. To prepare: the bulbs are washed and the outer husk or coat removed. They can be eaten raw, with salt to flavor, and have a pleasant starchy taste somewhat like a raw potato. The bulbs can be boiled for 15-30 minutes, or they can be fried or baked as one would potato tubers. They have a crisp nutlike texture, a pleasing flavor, and are one of our favorite native foods. We once placed 8-10 bulbs on a 12-inch pizza pie and cooked the mixture about 20 minutes with good success. Other special uses of the bulbs will occur to the experimental cook. The only drawback to the use of these plants, other than the difficulty of finding enough bulbs, is the fact that they are beautiful plants and using the underground parts might tend to eradicate them. For this reason we think that they should be used sparingly if at all, except in times of emergencies. The bulbs can be stored for future use should this be necessary.

Species:

About 40 species are recorded for the West, many of them limited to the Pacific Coast area. Of the 2 illustrated *C. nuttallii* is more widely distributed.

Camassia spp.
CAMASS, BLUE CAMASS, WILD HYACINTH

Description:

Plants from onionlike bulbs these sometimes over an inch
wide, usually with blackish coats but white inside; stems about
1 to 2 feet tall; leaves narrow and grasslike; flowers in a narrow
cluster; each flower 6-parted, blue-purple in color, each segment
about ⅜ to 1 inch long; fruit a short dry pod (capsule).

These plants grow from western Canada to California, east
to Utah and Montana.

Use:

These plants were an important food source of the Indians.
It has been reported that many local Indian wars were fought
over the collecting rights to certain meadows where camass hap-
pened to be abundant. The only drawback was that bulbs of
the death camas often grew on similar sites and apparently were
sometimes mixed in by mistake, often with fatal results. (Check
Zigadenus spp.) This could occur particularly if the collections
were made after the flowers had dropped. (The camass has blue
flowers, but the death camas has whitish to cream-colored ones).

One reads conflicting accounts of just when the bulbs were
collected, but apparently they are edible at any season. It is
better to take them in flower when the plants are conspicuous
and readily identified, but we have used them when the pods
were almost full sized. The Indians sometimes boiled the bulbs
down to form a syrup, but usually baked them in pits with the
"fireless cooker" method they so often used. The pit was dug
according to the amount of material (perhaps 6-10 feet wide and
2-3 feet deep) and lined with stones. Then a fire was built inside
and stones allowed to get very hot. The stones were then covered
with a layer of grass or other vegetation, the bulbs placed in the
pit, covered with another layer of grass and finally with dirt.
Sometimes water was poured on the mass, with a hole left for the

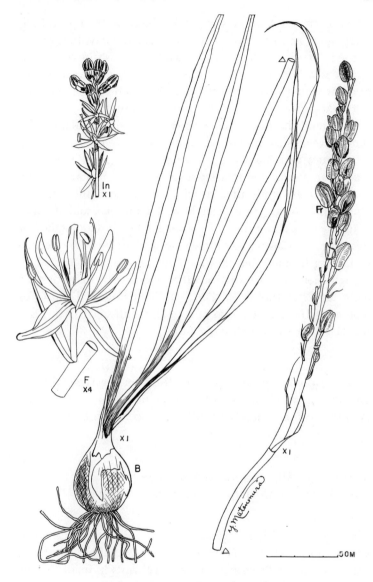

COMMON CAMASS (*Camassia quamash*)

steam to escape. A fire was sometimes built on the top to keep things good and hot. After from 12 hours to 3 days the pit was opened. The bulbs came out brown or blackish in color, and apparently were rich in sugar content. They were eaten at once or allowed to dry for storage. The bulbs could also be pounded into cakes which could be sun-dried for future use.

We found the raw bulbs were crisp and quite palatable although we must admit not exceptionally so. We boiled them for 25 minutes and found them pleasant tasting, but they were somewhat gummy and mucilaginous, annoying us somewhat by sticking to the teeth after chewing. We roasted the bulbs in aluminum foil at 350 degrees F. for 45 minutes and thought that they were about the same as boiled. The Indian method of steaming and roasting sounds best to us. Camass bulbs seem to be lacking in starch but they are high in sugar content and although their actual nutritive value may not be exceptionally high, they certainly remain an important potential source of food available over a period of several months of the year. But best beware of the death camas bulbs!

Species:
Only 2 similar species have been listed for the West with the one illustrated (*Camassia quamash*) being the most widely distributed, so that it has been called the "common camass."

Scirpus (the tall, round-stemmed species)
TULE BULRUSH, COMMON TULE, GREAT BULRUSH

Description:
Plants perennial, spreading by thick scaly (at least when young) rootstocks, these bearing relatively thick true roots; stems thick, 4-12 feet tall; flowers and seedlike fruits in small clusters (spikes), these usually many on each stem.

TULE BULRUSH *(Scirpus acutus)*

Plants found in wet ground or shallow water. Widespread in Canada and the United States, often at lower elevations in the West.

Use:

The Indians used these plants very extensively. In the spring they gathered the young shoots which were just coming up, and ate them raw or cooked. They are described as being white, crispy, juicy and nourishing. Even later in the season the base of the stems provided palatable, if somewhat tougher, chewing. When the bulrush was in flower the pollen was collected and often mixed with meal to make bread, mush or pancakes. Later on the seeds could be beaten off into baskets or pails, ground into a similar meal and used in the same fashion as the pollen. In the fall there might even be a new growth of young shoots ready for the taking. The old stems were used to weave into mats or baskets. The scaly rootstocks were available in all seasons of the year. They were eaten either raw or cooked; sometimes they were dried thoroughly in the sun, then pounded into a kind of flour. The Indians made a sweet syrup by bruising the root-stocks, boiling them for several hours (some writers say up to 15), then pouring off the sweet liquid. Certainly this was an important food plant to many Indian tribes.

We like the younger rootstocks best, the ones ending in new buds. These were peeled and eaten raw; they had no pronounced taste which was good or bad, but appeared to us to be nourishing. Yanovsky & Kingsbury found that one species (*Scirpus validus*) had as much as 8% sugar and 5.5% starch in its rootstocks, but less than 1% protein. We found that even the older rootstocks could be eaten raw although they were a bit fibrous.

We also peeled the rootstocks and boiled them for 30 minutes (5,000 feet), eating them with salt, pepper and butter. We concluded they made a very satisfactory dish. Tule bulrush seems to

us to be one of the very best survival plants we have in our area.
It is often locally very abundant and the parts are relatively
bulky. For example, the rootstocks can be almost 1 inch in
diameter; the only disadvantage is that they do require some
arduous digging. Various edible portions of the plant are available throughout every season of the year. There is no need to
go hungry in any season, even in winter, if a swamp is nearby
where bulrushes grow.

Species:

Around 20 species of *Scirpus* have been recorded for the West
but the 2 species of tall round-stemmed ones (*S. acutus* and
S. vallidus) are common and both widely distributed.

Claytonia spp.
SPRING BEAUTY

Description:

Plants sometimes from underground, tuberlike structures up
to 1½ inches thick, (corms) or else from long, thick, fleshy
purple-red taproots (as shown in the illustrations); stems short;
leaves mostly basal, these larger than the two on the stem, from
nearly round to rather narrow; petals white to pink in color,
each about ¼ to ½ inches long.

Rich soil, often along valleys, sometimes in partial shade or
on slopes and rockslides, from low to high elevations. Scattered
throughout the West.

Use:

A. *Corms* (like *C. lanceolata*)

The tuberous corms were much used by the Indians and
seem to us to be rather high in starch. When eaten raw they

WESTERN SPRING BEAUTY (*Claytonia lanceolata*)
AND ALPINE SPRING BEAUTY (*Claytonia megarrhiza*)

were crisp like potatoes, not at all displeasing but not very flavorful to our taste. We boiled them for 25 minutes (at 5,100 feet), some peeled and some with the jackets left on. The peeled ones were somewhat like potatoes, perhaps even better tasting. The peel came off readily on the whole ones after cooking, but we thought it imparted a slightly "earthy" taste to the contents. The spring beauty is an attractive spring flower, seldom growing abundantly and it does seem a shame to use the corms extensively except in real emergencies.

B. *Roots* (like *C. megarrhiza*)

We have eaten both the large taproots and the rosettes of leaves of those plants bearing them. The leaves, when eaten raw, are not displeasing but we must admit they are not particularly flavorful. However, we felt that they could be used to good advantage as a mixture in a salad.

The cooked young leaves, to our notion, made an acceptable potherb. We suggest boiling them for 10-15 minutes (at 5,000 feet elevation); the water does not need changing. We boiled the roots for 30 minutes. They tasted very nice except for that same "earthy" taste noted in the corms. We advise peeling the roots before cooking and suggest trying them baked. This plant should be an excellent survival plant if one were needed at higher elevations in the mountains.

Species:

Several species are present in the West but the 2 illustrated (*C. lanceolata* and *C. megarrhiza*) are the most common and most widely distributed. *C. virginica* and *C. caroliniana* are present in the eastern United States and produce edible corms. A far northern species, *C. tuberosa,* is used by the Eskimos according to report. Sometimes the genus *Claytonia* is united with *Montia* by botanists.

COMMON ARROWHEAD (*Sagittaria latifolia*)

Sagittaria spp.

ARROWHEAD, SWAMP POTATO, TULE POTATO, WAPATOO

Description:

These are variable plants in general habit, but are always perennial with long rootstocks that bear swollen tuberlike structures; the leaves may sometimes be ribbon-shaped but are usually arrow-shaped (as in the figure) with expanded parts (blades) up to 16 inches long; flowers medium to large in size, up to 1 inch wide, white in color; fruit a cluster of small seedlike structures.

Shallow water of streams and margins of lakes. Widespread in North America; in the West usually at lower to medium elevations.

Use:

The tubers are borne at the end of the slender rootstocks and may actually be located some distance from the main cluster of the stems of the parent plant. These tubers become much larger in the fall than is indicated in our drawing, and are said to reach the size of a man's fist. In our area we seldom get them larger than a hen's egg and they are often much smaller. They are solid and white-colored inside, covered with overlapping scales and are borne well below the soil surface, sometimes as much as a foot deep. This creates a problem when you attempt to collect an adequate supply. Arrowhead tubers were widely used by the North American Indians and the early explorers soon learned to eat them. For example, Lewis and Clark described how the Indian squaws waded into the water, sometimes up to breast-deep, dragging a canoe. The women would dig out the tubers with their toes, and the tubers, being light, would rise to the surface of the water to be collected later and thrown into the boat. The Indians would also raid muskrat caches in order to obtain a supply. Anyone in a bathing suit or hip boots, wielding a strong rake or potato fork, can obtain a good supply without too much labor.

Some people claim that these tubers can be eaten raw, but we have never cared for them that way. First, they have a distinctly bitter taste that may be unpalatable, although this seems to be more concentrated in the peeling. Even individual tubers seem to vary in the relative amount of this bitterness. Secondly, one may run a certain danger of contamination by eating them raw. We boiled them for about 15-30 minutes, removed the outer scales and ate them with salt, pepper and butter. We considered them excellent food, something on the order of potatoes, with little, if any, of the bitter taste remaining after cooking. We also roasted them for about 30-40 minutes at 375 degrees F., wrapped in aluminum foil, and liked them even better. The Indians often used their favorite pit method for cooking them. This is described by Mrs. Norton as follows:

Duck or Chicken and Wapatoo Imu

Wrap the duck or chicken (a leg of lamb will do) in some large leaves such as arrowhead. Wash the tubers. Dig a pit larger than the meat. Line this with stones about fist size and build a hot fire on them. When the stones are white hot, scrape out the embers, line the pit with a thick layer of grass or leaves, set the wrapped meat in place and surround with the arrowhead tubers. Cover with more leaves and grass, then a wet burlap sack and finally with warm earth from about the pit. After about one to two hours the pit may be opened and the meal served.

As has been suggested, arrowhead tubers would make a "superb" dish for a picnic supper. The guests can dig their own supply of tubers, wrap them in aluminum foil and roast them in a bed of hot coals if they don't care to use the fireless cooker or "imu" method.

The name "Wapatoo" apparently comes from the name of an island in or near the Columbia River where arrowheads grew in abundance, and were an important source of food to the Indians. This plant is much used in the Orient and certain species are said to be cultivated in China and Japan. Matsumura told us of its use in certain Japanese ceremonies:

1. New Year Ceremony

Boil the tubers for 10 minutes with a little salt. Discard the water and boil with soy sauce for 5-10 minutes.

2. Special Ceremony

Boil tubers as above, mix with 2 or 3 pieces of chicken, soy bean sauce or paste, mushrooms, carrots and burdock roots, stirred egg, soy sauce and sugar. Place in a bowl, cover it and put it in a steaming pan for 5 minutes. One would assume that the chicken, carrots and burdock roots were cooked first and some water or chicken stock was added as he stated that this produces a kind of soup called "Chawanmushi." This is apparently a semi-liquid product according to a statement of Oshima.

We followed Matsumura's suggestion of boiling the partly cooked tubers with a mixture of soy sauce and water; it did seem to improve the flavor somewhat. The Indians used to boil them, then string them up to dry for later use. We cut some of the raw tubers in slices and allowed them to dry in the sun. Some three years later we found them quite palatable when allowed to soak in the mouth, or when they were soaked in water for about an hour, then fried in butter. The bitter taste did persist to some degree and we concluded that the Indian method of drying the boiled tubers was superior. It has been reported that a flour can be obtained by grinding up these tubers.

The arrowhead plant is available for food throughout the whole year, even in winter if one is hardy enough or hungry enough to dig for it. The tubers are good boiled, fried or

roasted; in fact, in any way that potatoes are prepared; they
work in well with almost any other food. Certainly the arrowhead is well worth remembering in case of emergency, particularly since it is usually easy to recognize by the characteristic
leaf shape, and could hardly be mistaken for any harmful
plant.

Species:

The common arrowhead (*S. latifolia*) is, as the name suggests,
the most widespread one throughout North America and has
accordingly been selected to draw. About 4 other species seem
to be present in the West, the most of them having the
characteristic, arrow-shaped leaves.

Allium spp.
ONION, WILD ONION

Description:

Plants with the characteristic "onion" or "garlic" odor,
growing from underground scaly bulbs of varying size often
up to 1 inch wide; stems variable in height often up to 2 feet
long; leaves narrow and long, flat to nearly round in cross-
section; flowers in round or flat-topped clusters with the
individual flower stalks meeting at a common point (umbel—
see illustration), the cluster upright to nodding; individual
flowers white, whitish-rose or rose-purple, rather small in size.

The wild onions are widely distributed over the West usually
at low to medium elevations. They grow on plains, hills and
slopes, usually in rather open ground.

Use:

The wild onions can always be told by the flower cluster
(umbel), the underground bulb and the characteristic "onion"

ONION (*Allium cernuum & Allium geyeri*)

odor. This latter varies in strength and desirable quality among different species. Some observers, including the author, have noticed a fetid smell in some species which to us is definitely objectionable. This may partially disappear in the cooking process, and in our area wild onion species are definitely worth a trial by anyone. The Air Force Manual stated that wild onions are never poisonous. However, cultivated onions sometimes cause poisoning to likestock and any onion when grazed by milk cows may impart an "onion" or "garlic" flavor to the milk.

The bulbs or leaves of wild onions can be used as a flavoring for soups, stews and meats. The tops and bulbs can also be boiled or fried as the main food ingredient of the meal. General George Crook, on his "Starvation March" down the Yellowstone in 1876, said that wild onions formed a welcome addition to the food supply. It has been claimed that nodding onion (*A. cernuum*), and the eastern wild garlic (*A. canadense*), formed almost the entire food source of Marquette and his party on their journey from Green Bay, Wisconsin to the present site of Chicago in the fall of 1674. The juice of wild onions can be boiled down to a thick syrup, and has often been used as a cure for colds and throat irritations.

Wild onions can be used in place of their cultivated relatives in cooking, and for the same general purposes. Various recipes have been published for using them in salads, for frying them, for making soups, and for pickling the bulbs but anyone who uses the cultivated varieties much will have his own favorite methods of preparation for onions.

The Indians used wild onions extensively and apparently still do in many areas. They constitute both a readily identifiable and available emergency food. The bulbs can be dried and stored for future used should this be necessary. We have seen people out collecting wild onions and blithely gathering up bulbs of death camas with them! (See *Zigadenus*.) Such a mistake could be fatal.

Species:

Around 40 species of wild onions have been reported from the West. Naturally they are somewhat variable in general appearance but fortunately they all have the onion odor so that they can be identified even in the dark! The two illustrated (*A. cernuum* and *A. geyeri*) are widely distributed over our area.

Erythronium spp.
DOGTOOTH VIOLET, FAWNLILY, TROUTLILY, ADDER'S
 TONGUE

Description:

Plants with deep-seated tuberlike swellings (corms); stems usually less than 15 inches tall; leaves two on the stem, rather narrow but not grasslike; flowers one to several on each stem, medium in size, seldom over 1½ inches long, cream-colored to yellow or varying from white to pale purple or rose.

Ranges throughout the West often up to timberline in the mountains.

Use:

These characteristic and lovely plants are certainly too beautiful to gather indiscriminately as food. The leaves and corms can be used raw as a kind of salad, but they should be tried carefully as some writers say they have an emetic effect. The limited amounts we have tried had no such action. The young plants have been boiled as a potherb and are said to be good.

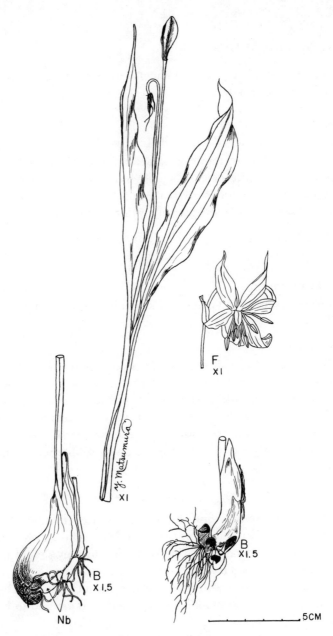

M. J. Matsumura

F
X1

B
X1.5

B
X1.5

Nb

5CM

DOGTOOTH VIOLET (*Erythronium grandiflorum*)

The corms are deep-seated and it is hard to dig out a reasonably sized mess. To make it worse they tend to snap off easily and may often be lost in the soil. They have a nice, crisp, chewy taste when eaten raw. We boiled them for varying times, but found 25 minutes (at 5,000 feet) to be about right. They had a very pleasant crisp taste and we like them very much. These plants are often locally abundant but the corms are hard to dig, and the plants are really too lovely to destroy. Consequently we must agree with practically everyone else on the subject who always advises that dogtooth violet should be used only in times of emergency. Remember, if you eat it raw, take it easy at first!

Species:

About a dozen species are listed for the West with the one illustrated (*E. grandiflorum*) being the most widely distributed one. Some of the species in the eastern United States have been used as edible ones for a long time.

Polygonum (*P. bistortoides* and *P. viviparum*)
BISTORT

Description:

Perennial from fleshy horizontal rootstocks; stems 4-28 inches tall, erect and unbranched; basal leaves up to 8 inches long, stem leaves shorter, each sheathing the stem at the base; flowers in a more or less elongated spikelike cluster ¾ to 1½ inches long and about ½ inch thick; individual flowers white to pale rose, small about ⅛ inch long, the lower ones often replaced by small bulblets.

Moist or wet meadows and swamps usually at rather high elevations in the mountains. Found all over the West.

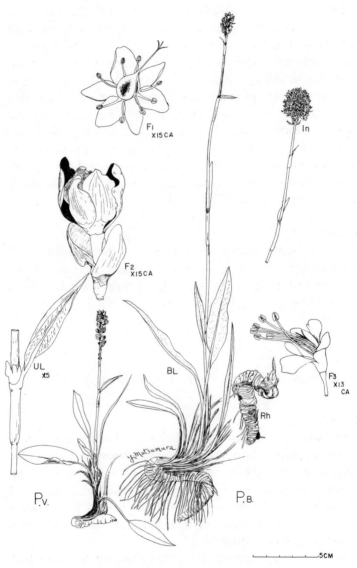

BISTORT (*Polygonum viviparum & bistortoides*)

Use:

For the two species: The two kinds have similar uses but the American Bistort (*P. bistortoides*) has the advantage of producing larger rootstocks. The young leaves can be used as a potherb and are said to have a pleasingly tart taste. The rootstocks have often been used by the Indians, some tribes esteeming them highly. We ate some of the rootstocks raw and thought them starchy and rather pleasant, with no bitter taste to the rind or contents. Some of the older ones were slightly fibrous and we would recommend cooking them. It does not seem necessary to peel them, which would be difficult to do in any case, since the surface is so rough and irregular. However, we must admit this peel does not improve the appearance of the cooked product.

We boiled them for 40 minutes and ate them with salt, pepper and butter, peel and all. The taste was rather starchy, but very pleasant. One of us compared the flavor to that of the water chestnut of Japan. We also wrapped the rootstocks in aluminum foil and baked them for 40 minutes in an oven at 300 to 325 degrees F. When eaten with butter, salt and pepper they were judged to be excellent food, with a sweet, pleasant, nutty taste.

Our two species are often abundant, the rootstocks are borne shallowly in the soil (although rather hard to dig), but they are fairly easy to secure in quantities; they are edible raw and are very palatable cooked. These plants would be excellent to try on a camping or fishing trip, and would make a good emergency food in the higher elevations in the mountains.

Species:

Some species of *Polygonum,* called "Smartweeds," have an acrid juice in the stems and leaves but these species all have two or more flower clusters to a stem and have only a distant resemblance to our two plants. Even some of these, such as

Polygonum persicaria, have been used as a salad or as a seasoning. The Japanese Knotweed (*P. cuspidatum*), with broad
leaves cut off square at the base, is often planted as an orna-
mental and sometimes runs wild, even becoming weedlike.
The young shoots have been cooked like asparagus and the
rootstocks boiled or baked.

The seeds of several kinds of *Polygonum* have been used as
food after being parched and ground into meal but they
would surely be tedious to gather in quantity.

Psoralea spp. (the species with thick tuberous roots)
BREADROOT, INDIAN POTATO, SCURFPEA

Description:

Plants perennial from swollen tuberlike roots; stems rather
stout, seldom much over a foot tall; leaf divisions (leaflets)
coming in to a common center; flower blue-tinged, each less
than 1 inch long, sweetpea shaped; fruit a short pod.

Prairies, plains and slopes. Scattered throughout the West.

Use:

The starchy, tuberlike roots furnished a well-known food to
the Indians, and the early white settlers soon discovered their
value. In fact, the roots of *P. esculenta* were sent back to
France in about the year 1800 by Lamare-Picquot, an early
explorer, with the expectation that the plant would become a
valuable cultivated crop. Although this fond hope did not
materialize, the breadroot has always been famous as a food
producer in this country and has sustained many a starving
person for a time. For example, John Colter, one of Lewis and
Clark's men, while escaping from the Blackfeet Indians, lived

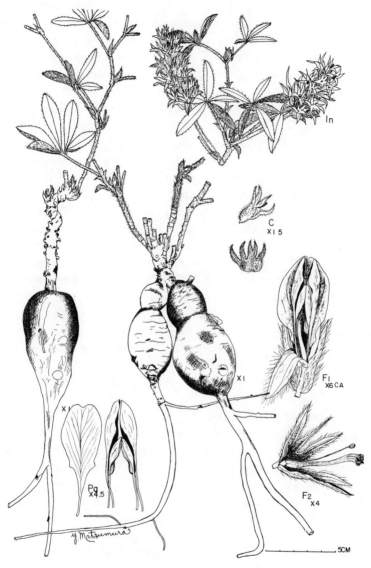

COMMON BREADROOT (*Psoralea esculenta*)

for a whole week entirely on the roots of breadroot. The Indians dug the roots in July or August when the tops were browning, peeled them, and cooked them in various ways. Sometimes they were dried in the sun and stored. They could later be ground into a meal for seasoning other food, thickening soup, making gruel or they were formed into cakes for making bread. In 1895, Havard had some of these roots analyzed. They contained 70% starch, 5% sugar and 9% nitrogenous matter. Subsequent analysis had a higher percentage of sugar and a lower one of starch, perhaps because of differences in the time of gathering.

We have found that the roots peeled easily, had a bright white inner core and a fairly thin outer covering. We consider that they are reasonably edible raw, rather tough to chew perhaps, but with no pronounced taste of any kind, certainly not a bad one. We boiled the roots in a pressure cooker to save time and gave them 30-40 minutes at 15 lbs. pressure. The taste was pleasant, being a mixture of nutlike and potato-like, but not at all strong flavored. We also roasted the root cores. These were wrapped in aluminum foil and placed for about 2 hours in an oven set at 375 degrees F. The taste was good but we thought they were somewhat better boiled.

We also cut some of the cores into thin slices, using a pocket knife, and let them dry on the window ledge. They certainly keep for any reasonable length of time, perhaps indefinitely, for 3 years later we soaked them in water for an hour and fried them in butter. They were slightly tough to chew as compared with fried potatoes, but had a pleasant, though not a pronounced taste.

These plants appear to us to be excellent edible species, particularly in times of emergency. The tuberous roots are fairly large, often being larger than a hen's egg. On the other hand, the plants do not seem to be very abundant, at least in our area, and it seems to us that they often grow in soil that is so hard that it is difficult to dig out the roots. Also, the taste of the roots of some of the species may not strike your fancy.

Species:

The species illustrated (*P. esculenta*) is the best known one although it comes into the eastern part of our area only. About 7 others have been reported but as indicated some of them do have a bitter taste or an unpleasant odor to us. At least none of them have been reported as poisonous.

Perideridia spp.
WILD CARAWAY, YAMPA, SQUAWROOT

Description:

Plants from solitary more or less thickened roots or from clusters of such roots; stems up to 4 feet tall; leaves divided into narrow segments; flowers white, small, in compound clusters (umbels), the individual stalks arising from a common center; fruits small, resembling caraway.

Meadows, valleys and mountain slopes in open or partially shaded ground. Throughout the West.

Use: (mostly of *P. gairdneri*)

This was a favorite root food among the Indians, often mentioned as the one they liked the best. This is not surprising to us, as it is also one of our favorite edible native plants. The roots tend to taper both ways, are rather small in size (⅝ of an inch in diameter being a good-sized one) and are covered with a thin brown skin. The plant is abundant only

YAMPA (*Perideridia gairdneri*)

in local areas, as for example in the drainage valley of the Yampa River in northwestern Colorado. The Indians were said to have swarmed into that area each fall to gather the roots of what they called "Yampa." The plant gave its name to the whole valley, the river that flows through it, and the town of Yampa. In fact, it has been pointed out that when several names were considered for the proposed new state, the name "Yampa" ran close competition with the finally selected "Colorado."

The Indians were said to have gathered the roots and placed them in baskets in running water. Then the squaws would tread them with bare feet to remove the outer skin. This sounds like one of the well-known wine-making stories. The early pioneers, notably Lewis and Clark and John Fremont, learned the value of this plant from the Indians. Even today many people in the West make at least a limited use of the plant. We have tried these roots in many ways and they seem to get better every time we eat them. They have a sweet, nutty, parsnip-like flavor when eaten raw, with a percentage of sugars that equals or surpasses the starch content. As one of us remarked, "They taste like parsnips—if parsnips only tasted good."

The outer peel is thin and we have found it unnecessary to remove it. We have cooked the roots by several methods. They were boiled for 25 to 35 minutes (at 5,000 feet), depending on their size, and it was found that the peeling separated readily if this is desired. We usually ate them with butter, pepper, and just a little salt. They were very good, but it is our feeling that some of the sweet taste is removed in the boiling process. The leftover boiled roots can also be fried. We liked the roots when baked in a 350 degree F. oven for 40 minutes. They were crisp, sweet and tender with a delicious taste. In fact, any of the many recipes for cooking ordinary potatoes would certainly work for wild caraway roots. Here are two we liked:

CREAMED WILD CARAWAY

Make about 1 cupful of sauce using:

1 tablespoon butter or other	¾ teaspoon salt
shortening	1/16 teaspoon pepper
2 tablespoons flour	1 cup milk

Melt butter, add flour, salt and pepper and mix well. Add milk slowly and bring to the boiling point, stirring constantly to avoid lumps. Stir in about 1 cup of cut up, boiled and peeled wild caraway roots.

CANDIED WILD CARAWAY

Heat some butter with brown sugar and drop in whole, boiled, peeled roots. Then stir over a fire until they are coated or candied. The taste may be almost too sweet for some palates and an addition of some orange juice might be good.

We found the roots dried readily in the sun, either whole or when split longitudinally. The dried product seems to keep indefinitely, but we have found this difficult to do because several of us around the laboratory have formed the habit of nibbling on them. We let the pieces soak up in the mouth a bit before chewing; the flavor is aromatic and sweet. The sliced roots, when soaked in water for half an hour and when fried in butter, have a taste we would describe as "sweet, tender and good." The Indians were said to grind up the roots to form a sort of meal which could be used in various ways. Wild caraway is a close relative of cultivated caraway and the seeds (fruits) have also been used in seasoning.

This plant is locally abundant, the roots are easy to dig, they do not need peeling, they are delightful tasting raw or cooked, and they dry readily for storage. On the other hand they are rather small, do not store well in fresh, undried condition like potatoes, our experience makes us suspect they are not so palatable during their active growing season, and lastly, they belong to the same family as some deadly poisonous plants (like *Conium maculatum* and *Cicuta douglasii*). Of course they do have some superficial resemblance to them. However, the resemblance is not very close and this is surely one of our best edible plants. If the roots could be enlarged by selection or breeding surely wild caraway roots could be cultivated and marketed. What a shame that this delicious taste sensation has been almost lost to mankind!

Species:

We have about 8 species scattered throughout the West but *P. gairdneri* (the one illustrated), is the most widespread and the best known as an edible plant.

Chapter II: LEAVES AND SHOOTS
(like Spinach and Asparagus)

THE YOUNG TENDER LEAVES or the juvenile shoots of many wild plants are often variously cooked (usually boiled) and called "potherbs" or "greens." Sometimes they are used raw as a salad, usually with the addition of some type of dressing. Most of us like this dressing to be a highly seasoned one since so many of our native plants have a somewhat "wild" taste.

In all such cases the practical problem is how to be absolutely certain as to the identification of these plants in the young condition, for many edible plants at this stage do have a superficial resemblance to harmful ones. There are no flowers or fruit present to aid in this checking and the young plants may look much different than the mature familiar forms. You may have watched certain of these juvenile plants grow into these mature forms in previous years and by "remembering backwards" you can sometimes proceed with assurance.

Also sometimes a few precocious individuals flower extra early and these plants can be more easily identified. Then the slower maturing ones can be utilized with safety. An even better method for the serious student is suggested below in the steps listed:

1. Collect and dry (by pressing) some of the young plants in "salad" or "greens" condition. Directions for pressing plants are given in Harrington's *How To Identify Plants.*

2. Allow other plants of the same kind to mature to form flowers or fruit.

3. Identify (or have identified) these dried pressed mature plants.

4. Mount the juvenile and mature pressed plants preferably together on a cardboard. You are now ready for next season.

5. Next year compare the young fresh plants with this pressed material.

Here are some general suggestions for the use of these young parts based both on our own and upon the experience of others.

1. If at all possible use only the young tender parts. Of course, the age and tenderness will affect any necessary cooking time. Remember that your elevation above sea level will do the same; boil them longer at high altitudes. The best advice we can give is to experiment a bit, using common sense in the matter. *Never overcook* is a good rule for greens.

2. Usually springtime is the season for gathering greens or salads, but remember our summer rains will often germinate the seeds of annual plants or cause a perennial one to push out its young shoots.

3. Some species have a rather sharp or bitter taste that is objectionable to some people, especially when it is first experienced. You can overcome this to some degree by changing the water two to several times during the boiling process or by using a robust dressing on your salad. Also, many of us like to mix these piquant plants with others having a bland taste.

4. The rule is to use as little water as possible in cooking and change it only when necessary. This water can be saved to drink or it can be used in cooking other foods. Some of the minerals and vitamins may be lost if you pour the water away. Of course, in times of acute water shortage this cooking liquid may be very valuable.

5. Large underground parts of many plants can be brought in to the cellar and buried in soil. Such structures can provide a supply of fresh greens or salads at intervals throughout the winter.

6. Patches of growing plants can be covered from several days

to several weeks with burlap, thick paper boxes, or inverted tubs. The lack of light causes rapid elongation of the stems, the parts become yellowish or whitish (blanched), more tender, usually less bitter. This is what is done commercially to several garden plants, such as celery.

7. Some wildland greens are rather lacking in pronounced flavor and taste. If you find them so, then doctor them up with diced bacon, salt pork, or hard boiled eggs, using your favorite recipe for spinach.

8. The problem of contamination by sprays, bacteria, organic material, various insect stages, animal parasites, etc., is very serious especially with the salads which are eaten raw. The leaves or shoots should always be washed in clean water. Some folks dissolve a halazone tablet in water and soak the salad material in this.

Potherbs properly cooked and fresh salads are considered to be relatively high in vitamins. They are rather seasonable, but when available are usually so in very large quantities. They do seem to be relatively low in actual nutrients. It is possible to can, freeze, or dehydrate greens and keep them for rather long periods, but the possibilities in this respect seem to us to be somewhat limited. Many of them are high in flavor and palatability (at least to some of us), often much more so than their cultivated counterparts.

Taraxacum spp.
DANDELION

Description:

Plants perennial from taproots; the fresh parts exuding a sticky milky juice when cut or broken; true stems very short, the leaves clustered at about ground level; leaves lobed in from

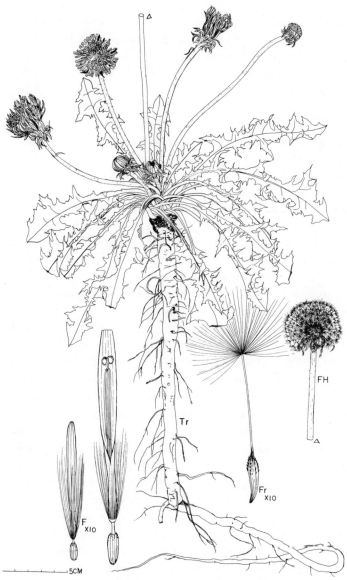

COMMON DANDELION (*Taraxacum officinale*)

their sides; leafless flower stalks (not true stems) hollow in the center, varying in height depending on where the plant grows, elongating in age, up to 1 foot long; individual flowers many but crowded into a single head (which appears as one flower), this yellow and about $\frac{1}{2}$ to 2 inches wide; fruits small and seedlike, each one bearing a parachute of hairs at the apex.

Almost throughout the world. Lawns, pastures and meadows sometimes even above 10,000 feet elevation in the mountains. A very common weed.

Use:

The dandelion is a plant of many uses in many corners of the globe. The seeds have often been deliberately carried from place to place for cultivation. This accounts, at least in part, for its wide distribution. The seedlike fruits can be carried long distances on air currents since each one bears a very efficient parachute of hairs. Many people consider (or pretend to consider) that the bright yellow dandelion flowers are attractive on their lawn, and they may be right. However, the effect is marred later on when they form their globular heads of gray or white fruits which are quickly elevated above the surrounding grass. Other people wage a constant battle against them and use every method they can think of to clear them off the place. Some use various chemical preparations, like 2-4D, to spray on the plants. It is wise to avoid such sprayed dandelions in collecting them for food. It has been observed by many people that the prevailing winds always blow from a lawn well spotted with the yellow and gray dandelion heads toward a lawn where such a constant eradication battle is being waged!

The young dandelion leaves are fancied by many in a salad. As they age they not only toughen but take on a decidedly bitter taste that is displeasing to many people. We always look around for plants in the shade or for those that have been covered with sand or litter. Such plants may be naturally blanched and the yellow or whitish leaves are then at their best. If you wish, you can blanch the plants yourself by covering them with cans, pots, straw, or canvas. A clever arrangement is to dig up a supply of the roots and put them in earth in flower pots or boxes. These can be carried into the basement and later on, often during the winter, will supply you with an amazing amount of blanched leaves. Try the young, preferably blanched leaves, in a salad with onions, radishes, parsley, and a little sugar. We also like them tossed with diced hard boiled eggs, with vinegar and oil. Some people find it easier to slice off the top of the crown with its attached leaves when collecting material; this crown top may be left on if you wish. We have used clusters of fresh leaves in Japanese Tempura with delicious results.

The young leaves are a favorite food when boiled as a potherb. When the leaves are tender or blanched you may not have to change the water in the process, but we have found that 2 or 3 changes are usually necessary to eliminate or cut down the bitter taste. In general, dandelion greens can be used as you would spinach, dressed up with crisp fried bacon or hard boiled eggs, creamed, in soups, scalloped or baked with meats, etc. If you find them strong tasting, try mixing them with other blander greens (see *Amaranthus* species). We boiled them for 10-20 minutes depending on the age of the leaves.

The roots are said to be sliced and used in salads by some people. They are also roasted, fried or when dried and ground, made into a coffee-like beverage much as chicory is used. We have tried them and decided they have a distinctive taste that might take a bit of getting used to before becoming pleasurable. We have heard that the dried leaves can be used to make a kind of "tea"; we have seen dandelion tea for sale in a local grocery store.

You might try the blossoms with pancakes. Use the young

heads and drop them on the top of the pancake batter on the frying pan. When the pancake is turned over the heads are cooked and will add variety and color to your camp breakfast. The blossoms are famous for wine making and several recipes for making it have been published. We give a representative one below:

DANDELION WINE

1 gallon dandelion petals	4 lbs. sugar
1 gallon boiling water	1 yeast cake (compressed)
4 oranges	1 lb. chopped raisins
1 lemon	1 slice toast

Pick the flowers from the heads, throwing away the hollow stalks and the denuded heads. Place them in a crock or jar and pour the boiling water over them.

Cover and leave for about 5 days, stirring several times during that period if you wish.

Strain out the liquid and add the sugar to it. Peel the oranges and lemon and drop in the peel, then add the juices of these fruits and the chopped raisins. Boil all this for 20 minutes in a preserving kettle and return it to the crock. Cool, place the yeast on the piece of toast and put it in. Cover and leave for about 3 days. Then decant the liquid into jars or bottles. Some say that the wine should be aged for at least one year before using.

A final use of dandelions was given to us by Bagdonas. He stated that the Boy Scouts of this area eat the seedlike fruits raw as an emergency food. The plumelike hairs are grasped by the fingers and the fruits are readily broken off and eaten. Sometimes these have a slight bitter taste, but not enough to make them distasteful in times of acute food shortage. This plant is certainly a valuable edible plant, and since it is abundant at all elevations, it is a valuable all around source of food. It is said to be very high in vitamins A and C.

Species:

The species illustrated (*T. officinale*) is probably the most common one throughout the West. It has pale gray to olive-green seedlike fruit. The similar *T. laevigatum* (once known as *T. erythrospermum*) with reddish colored fruit is found occasionally with it. In addition we have several, less common native species of dandelion in the West that should be tried for their edible qualities.

Asclepias speciosa
MILKWEED, SHOWY MILKWEED, SILKWEED

Description:

Plants in patches with thick spreading rootstocks; stems with milky juice, erect, stout, $1\frac{1}{3}$ to 5 feet tall at maturity; leaves opposite on the stems, oblong to narrowly egg-shaped with characteristic veins (as shown in the illustration), rather thick; flowers in globose clusters (umbels); individual flowers up to $\frac{1}{2}$ inch long or more, pink to light rose in color; fruit a pod about 3 to 5 inches long at maturity with soft finger-like processes on the surfaces.

Common at low to medium elevations throughout the West.

Note: Some of the milkweed species are poisonous to livestock. Better stick to the one described and illustrated.

Use:

This milkweed has actually been listed as possibly causing poisoning to livestock, but animals certainly seldom eat it. For this reason, we do not recommend this plant to be used raw in salad preparations. But properly prepared this is one of our most enjoyable and versatile edible species, and is one of our own favorite foods. The very young shoots can be prepared and

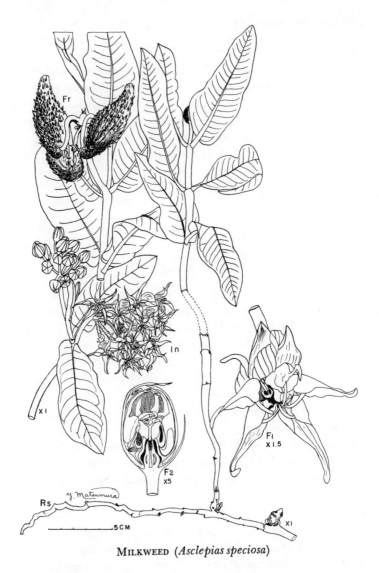

MILKWEED (*Asclepias speciosa*)

cooked like those of asparagus. They are best gathered when they are about 4 to 8 inches above the ground level. We boiled them for about 15-20 minutes, changing the water one or two times. This is a good procedure in cooking any part of the milkweed plant as it helps get rid of the bitter taste of the milky juice. The shoots can be eaten like asparagus, creamed or with butter; we think that they are very tender and palatable. They taste as good or even better than asparagus to most palates, and have the advantage of being much more abundant in most localities. Sometimes they may not be very tender and may require longer cooking than given above. These shoots are very good in Japanese Tempura batter and taste almost the same as asparagus.

If the shoots get too far along, the tender tops can be collected or, in any event, the younger leaves near the expanding terminal bud. These can be cooked like spinach, changing the water as mentioned before but probably boiling them for a longer period because the milkweed parts are a bit tougher than the garden vegetable. If you miss them in this stage, the flower buds can be gathered before they open and boiled for about 12-15 minutes with several changes of water. We have tried them with salt, pepper and butter and found them delicious. The taste is somewhat like peas or asparagus but with a flavor all its own. We have heard that the flower clusters are so full of sugar that they can be boiled down to make a thick syrup.

If you come along too late for the flowers, you can use the young pods when they are about 1 to 1½ inches long. They may remind you of okra, but when boiled make an appetizing dish. Norton suggested cooking them with rice and appropriate seasonings.

The Indians often cooked parts of the milkweed with meat with the idea that a substance in the plant had a tenderizing effect. It is too bad that certain related milkweeds cause serious poisoning to livestock but fortunately these species are not too hard to tell from the edible ones. The broad-leaved milkweed is almost a "pantry in the wild," and surely no one should go hungry while it is in the earlier stages of its growth. Even after

the pods mature the downy seeds can be gathered and used to
stuff sacks that serve as pillows or mattresses. Surely this is one
of our most useful plants.

Species:

Some 25 species have been reported from the West, varying
greatly in leaf shape and flower color. The one illustrated (*A.
speciosa*) is common and widely distributed. A related edible
species, *A. syriaca* is common in the eastern part of the United
States.

Agave spp.
AGAVE, MESCAL, CENTURY PLANT, MAGUEY

Description:

Plants with short vertical stems or rootstocks (not flowering
stalks) on which are crowded the many basal leaves; leaves
evergreen, rather narrow, spiny on the margins; flower stalks
arising from the center of the leaf cluster, often up to 10 feet
tall or more; flowers in narrow to broad clusters, whitish to
yellow, or tinged with red or purple, each one often up to 2
inches long, the swollen ovary borne below the segments (ovary
inferior); fruit a dry capsule. The plants resemble species of
Yucca (see *Y. baccata*), but have spiny instead of fibrous leaf
margins.

Scattered over the southern and southwestern parts of the
West, on arid slopes and deserts.

Use:

The smaller agaves and the larger southern ones were at one
time extensively utilized by the Indians for food and drink.
They were used at any time, but especially when the flower

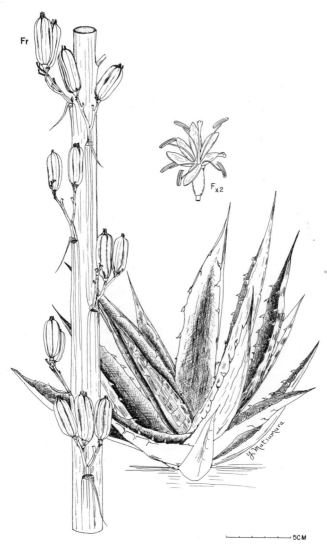

Fr

F_{x2}

5CM

AGAVE (*Agave utahensis*)

stalks were just arising from the leaf clusters. The centers of
the plants were dug out by using a pry-shaped piece of wood.
These centers contained the buds, short stalks, and some of

the leaf bases; the whole structure in the larger species of agave was said to be up to 2 feet in diameter. These were placed in circular pits about 6 to 20 feet in diameter and 1 to 2 feet deep. Stones were placed in the pit and a fire was laid upon them. The mescal butts were then placed in the pit, covered with grass or weeds, and finally with dirt. The plants were roasted in this way for 1 to 3 days. The product had a pleasantly sweet taste but contained fibers that had to be spit out when chewed. It could be pounded flat and dried in the sun in thin sheets and transported long distances as a future food supply. The roasted material could be soaked in water and a drink prepared by fermentation of the liquid. Also the large southern species have been treated by boring a cavity in the center of the plants and taking the sap out. This was fermented and often distilled, the resulting product being called "mescal, pulque, or tequila." The Mescalero Apaches owe their name to their use of this plant; the presence of the old roasting pits throughout the Southwest testify as to the past importance of agave in the diet of the Indians.

This plant can be a possible emergency food since it can be used at any time. The bud or center of the plant can readily be pried out by anyone, and roasted in pits or in the ashes of a fire. The resulting product can then be dried, if necessary, and used as sustenance on the journey to safety. Digging out the bud does not necessarily kill the plant as it may reproduce by offsets clustered around the parent. Of course, the presence of the flower stalk indicates that the primary leaf cluster producing it will soon die anyway. However, it seems better to us to consider this plant as an emergency food only.

The leaves of many species of agave contain a fiber that can be utilized in making twine or rope, and some kinds are cultivated for that purpose in parts of Mexico. The seeds have been ground up and used as food. Several writers have suggested that at least some species of agave contain laxative or irritants, especially when eaten in too large amounts, so it would be well to try this food product with reasonable care at first.

Species:

About 10 species have been recorded from the West, some with narrow, some with broad flower clusters. The species illustrated (*A. utahensis*), not withstanding its local name, ranges from southern California to southern Utah.

Capsella bursa-pastoris
SHEPHERD'S PURSE

Description:

Annual (or winter annual) plants; stems erect or nearly so, 4 inches to over a foot long in favorable sites; leaves tending to cluster near the base of the plants, at least in the young stages; petals white and small, only about 1/24 inch long; pod of characteristic triangular shape, ¼ to ¾ inch long.

A weed in waste places, gardens, lawns, and fields, now widely distributed throughout the United States. Like all weeds it can be locally very abundant.

Use:

This plant has a variety of uses and has actually appeared for sale on the markets in the eastern part of the United States. The ripening fruits were sometimes gathered, dried, and the seeds beaten out. These were ground into a meal by the Indians, but it would require a bit of patience to secure an adequate amount. The pods and seeds can be used to flavor

Fr ×10 CA

In ×2

F ×30

5 CM

SHEPHERD'S PURSE (*Capsella bursa-pastoris*)

other foods such as vegetable soup, and can be dried and stored for fall and winter.

The young leaves may be eaten raw in salads, especially if they are blanched. This can be done by covering a patch of the plants with straw, boards or canvas for a week or more. The fresh or dried roots have been utilized as a substitute for ginger, and have been candied by boiling in a rich sugar syrup. However, the widest use of shepherd's purse is as a pot-herb. We boiled the young leaves for 20 minutes and changed the water once. This change, however, may not be necessary. We ate the plant with a little salt and vinegar and found it somewhat stronger than spinach but with none of the bitter peppery taste reported by some people. In fact, we rated it better than spinach with a background taste of cabbage or Brussels sprouts. The Boy Scouts of the area rate it second only to dandelion as a food plant.

This is a plant easy to identify and easy to collect in reasonable quantities. It might well be tried in moderate quantities at first or mixed with other plants in salads or greens until one is sure it will be relished alone.

Species:

Only one species.

Montia perfoliata (Claytonia perfoliata, Limnia perfoliata)
MINER'S LETTUCE, INDIAN LETTUCE

Description:

Annual plants with sprawling stems about 2-6 inches long or more; leaves of two types, basal long-stalked, only 2 stem leaves present, these inserted opposite and their bases partly or completely joined to each other; petals $\frac{1}{8}$ to $\frac{1}{4}$ inch long, white to pink.

Moist banks and slopes, often in partial shade. This plant

5 CM

MINER'S LETTUCE (*Montia perfoliata*)

is found throughout the West, east to the Black Hills of South
Dakota and Utah.

Use:

This was a well-known food plant to the Indians and to the

early white settlers. It was reported to have been cultivated in France; also our Indians may have cultured or at least encouraged its growth in their immediate area.

In the spring the young plants may be used raw as a kind of salad. The shoots and leaves can also be cooked as "greens" and are reported to be excellent. The two contrasting kinds of leaves makes it a plant easy to recognize and it was very popular during the gold rush to California, hence the name "miner's lettuce." It was one of the fresh native plants that could be used to cure and avert scurvy.

Species:

About a dozen other species are present in the West, some of them like *M. chamissoi* are worth a trial. *M. siberica* has been used as food in Alaska. The genus *Montia* is often merged with *Claytonia* by botanists.

Salsola spp.
RUSSIAN THISTLE, TUMBLEWEED, SALTWORT

Description:

Annual, much-branched plants, forming roundish masses 1 to 3 feet or more in diameter that act as "tumbleweeds"; leaves 1 to 2½ inches long, becoming spiny-pointed at maturity; flowers inconspicuous; fruit seedlike, bearing horizontal, papery wings.

Dry plains, fields, roadsides, and waste places, often acting as a weed. This plant has been introduced from Eurasia in various parts of the United States, especially in the western half. It is now common at low to medium elevations, seldom occurring above 8,500 feet in the mountains.

TUMBLEWEED *(Salsola kali)*

Use:

The young, rapidly growing shoots, around 2 to 5 inches tall, make a very good potherb. We clipped off the roots and boiled the tops for 12-15 minutes without a change of water. Served like spinach with salt, pepper, and butter, or with the addition of vinegar or lemon juice, we found Russian thistle plants mild, pleasant, and crisp tasting, making them one of the very best potherbs we have ever eaten. They can be dressed up with fried bacon strips or hard boiled egg slices as you would serve spinach, but are also good stirred into a cream sauce and served over toast. Because of the bland taste they can be mixed to good advantage with other more "tangy" plants such as mustard.

We try to collect the young plants soon after a good rain, when the parts are tender and succulent. In most years they are not available for a very long period of the year, although there may be several of these young stages during some seasons depending on the rainfall pattern. Russian thistle is remarkably resistant to drought and a light rain may bring up the young plants, which can quickly mature in dry periods. These young plants have been mowed and used as an emergency hay crop for livestock in this area. Russian thistle is available in almost unlimited quantities during its limited tender period; it certainly should be utilized more often. The seeds are abundant and might be collected, ground into a meal, and eaten in an emergency. They might be rather hard to secure in quantity since the mature plant is so spiny. Carpenter and Steggerda found that the seeds contained 3.9 calories per gram.

Species:

The common species in the area is *S. kali* var. *tenuifolia* but a closely related one, *S. collina,* has been reported and should be just as edible, especially since it may not be as spiny.

AMARANTH (*Amaranthus retroflexus*)

PROSTRATE PIGWEED (*Amaranthus graecizans*)

Amaranthus spp. (mainly *A. retroflexus & A. graecizans,*
the ones illustrated)
AMARANTH, PIGWEED, REDROOT, CARELESS WEED

Description:
Annual plants with a taproot that is often reddish in color;
stems erect or prostrate; leaves with margins smooth to somewhat toothed, often egg-shaped and connected at the wide or
the narrower end; flowers inconspicuous, often minutely
bristly, either in terminal clusters or in the axils of the leaves;

seeds lens-shaped, black and shining, very small, up to 1/25 inch wide.

Common weeds, often in crops, along roadsides or on disturbed ground. They are widely distributed over North American and are widespread throughout the West but not common at high elevations in the mountains.

Use:

These plants have always been favorite ones among the Indians and were actually cultivated or at least encouraged by them to grow nearby. They used the small black seeds which are borne in surprising numbers. The mature plant can be stacked up on canvas or rock and allowed to dry, then the material shaken and beaten to shatter out the seeds. We placed the tops of these plants upside down in a large paper sack and let them dry for a week. Then the plants were shaken and beaten, the seeds and chaff remaining in the sack. The seeds were then separated using a sieve, and winnowed by the aid of a good breeze. The Indians parched the seeds and ate them whole, but they are so small it is difficult to chew up each one. They were also ground into a meal, often mixed with cornmeal and used in making bread, cakes, mush, or gruel. Soaking the seeds (or the meal) overnight in water may be a good idea according to our experience. The taste is some-what "weedy" to some people but pleasant enough even if the resulting product is rather blackish in color. However, a dark-colored pancake, bread, or mush might taste about as good as a light colored one to a hungry person. Certainly the seeds can be an emergency food of great importance. We have seen people shake out the seeds in their hands, throw them in their mouth and eat them raw.

The young shoots and stems have long been considered favorite material for greens by the Indians, the early white settlers, and by interested parties of recent times. They are

cooked like spinach. We cooked them 2 minutes at 15 lbs.
pressure in a pressure saucepan or boiled them for 12 minutes
in salted water (at 5,000 feet elevation). We have eaten them
with pepper and butter or with vinegar, bacon, or hard boiled
eggs. The flavor is rather mild but very pleasant and justifies
the popularity of this plant for greens. Some prefer to mix
these greens with those from plants having a more pronounced
flavor. The young plants may also be served raw as a salad.

Species:

We have about a dozen species of *Amaranthus* in the West
but they resemble more or less closely one of the two illustrated
(*A. retroflexus* and *A. graecizans*). The last one used to be
incorrectly called *A. blitoides* by the botanists.

Urtica spp.
NETTLE, STINGING NETTLE

Description:

Perennial plants with creeping underground rootstocks;
stems up to 6 feet tall (but usually 2-4) bearing stinging hairs
at least below; leaves 2 at one horizontal area on the stem
(opposite), fairly broad; flowers greenish-colored and inconspicuous.

Along streams, valleys, canyons, ditches or in waste places
where the ground is more or less moist. Widely distributed
throughout the West and throughout North America.

Use:

The nettle has always been popular as a food in other parts
of the world. The French are said to make at least seven kinds
of dishes from it; in Scotland it is as popular a potherb as it is

In.1
X3

In.2

F1

F2
X20

5 CM

X1

NETTLE (*Urtica dioica*)

in many other countries of Europe. The only drawback to its
use is the presence of stinging hairs which make gathering it a

problem. These stiff hairs are sharp but brittle at the ends and hollow in the center, this cavity leads down to a bulbous base that is filled with a stinging fluid, which is said to contain formic acid. If the tip of the hair is allowed to penetrate the skin, especially under pressure, the liquid is injected as if from a hypodermic needle.

We use gloves, preferably leather ones, when gathering nettles, or if we have forgotten the gloves we handle the young shoots carefully with the thumb and first two fingers to avoid letting them touch the tender skin of the hands. Even if we do get a few stings they are not serious (at least to us) and the effects soon pass away. Of course this sting is inactivated completely on cooking the plants.

The commonest use of nettle is as a potherb, cooked and used like spinach. We selected tender shoots about 6 to 8 inches tall. If these are pulled or dug up one finds a length of pink underground stem connecting them with the lower rootstock. These portions are tender and can be included with the tops. We boiled them for about 15 minutes with just enough water to cover the herb. They can be used to flavor or augment many other foods; we like them best when served with butter or vinegar. They have a bland taste of spinach and for that reason are often mixed with stronger tasting plants like sorrel or mustard. Cameron suggested the following recipe for soup.

NETTLE SOUP

Wash and boil the nettle shoots, then rub the parts through a sieve. Melt a little butter, sprinkle in an ounce of flour, add the nettles, and (a little at a time) sufficient milk to make a soup of the desired thickness. Bring to a boil, simmer for a few minutes, and season.

Nettle rootstocks can be dug in the fall, placed in a tub or box, and brought into the cellar. During the winter these will usually produce a supply of blanched tender shoots. Of course, during the growing season, the plants outside can be blanched by excluding the light in some manner from the developing shoots.

Nettles are said to be high in vitamin C and have been found by Storer to contain about 5.5% albuminoids and about 7.8% carbohydrates. They can be used to make a kind of "tea"; the directions usually given are to use 5 handfuls of nettle to 1 quart water. We have seen nettle tea for sale in this area. Nettles have also been used as a substitute for rennet, to coagulate milk.

A beer or wine may be made from nettles, using, in addition, dandelion flowers, lemon juice, ginger root, brown sugar, and yeast. We have not tried this out, but it is said to be good. Finally, the fibers of the mature stems can be retted out and spun into a durable cloth. Thomas Campbell, the British poet once said, "In Scotland I have eaten nettle, I have slept in nettle sheets, I have dined off a nettle tablecloth."

This is an excellent edible plant and makes an acceptable substitute for spinach. It is another plant that has the advantage of being easy to find and identify—even in the dark!

Species:

Just a few species are recorded for the West; they all look somewhat like the one illustrated here. *U. dioica* (in the broad sense) is common and widely distributed in North America.

Rumex spp.
DOCK, SORREL

Description:

(Includes only the two general types illustrated.)

Perennial plants from taproots or creeping rootstocks; stems

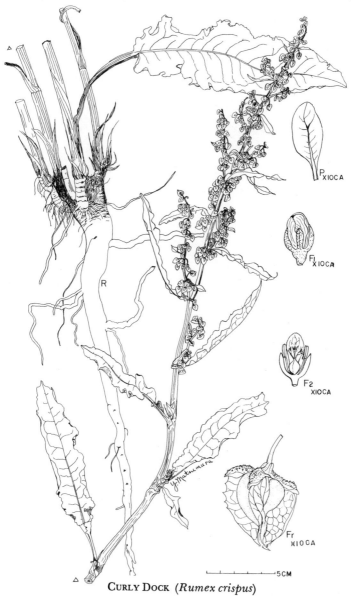

P x10CA

F₁ x10CA

F₂ x10CA

Fr x10CA

5CM

CURLY DOCK (*Rumex crispus*)

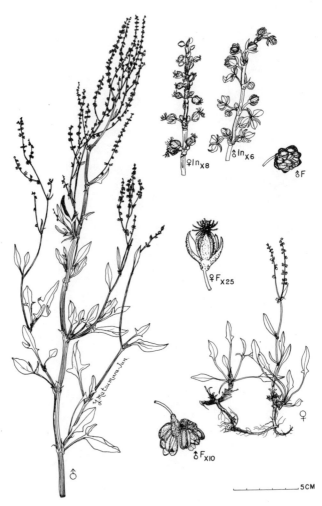

SHEEPSORREL (*Rumex acetosella*)

upright, often up to 4 feet tall; leaf stalks sheathing the stems
at the base, the margins often wavy or lobed near the base;

flowers small and inconspicuous; fruit seedlike with 3 wings, sometimes brightly colored.

Often in old fields, roadsides and waste places as weeds. Widespread throughout North America. In the West usually at low elevations but we have seen plants up to timberline in the mountains.

Use:

There are about 20 species of plants of this area that resemble the illustrations, and all are called "docks." All of them are edible to some degree, although some of them are not very pleasant tasting. They contain oxalates in varying amounts, and a few have caused losses to livestock when they are grazed upon them to excess. There has never been any difficulty reported with human beings; in fact, the docks and sorrels have always been famous food producers. Many people consider the curly dock to be the best of all the docks, and that is our own opinion at the present time. (See the illustration.)

We gathered the leaves in the spring while they were tender and free from insect holes. It was rather easy to secure abundant material, and this lost less bulk in cooking than would be expected. The large coarse leaves, upon cooking, became surprisingly tender. We have been told that a second crop of young leaves may be produced in the fall, particularly after a heavy rain. We boiled these young leaves for 10 minutes in limited liquid without changing water at all. Served with salt, pepper, and vinegar or lemon juice, like spinach, they proved to be very good. We have never noticed any real rank, bitter taste to most of these plants, but this is sometimes described in the literature, with the advice to change the cooking water several times. You can find this out by experiment. Many of the docks have a sour taste that led one Indian woman to observe, "It already has the vinegar in it." We consider the greens "bland" tasting and rather like them in mixtures with some others of a more pronounced taste, such as some of the mustards.

Soup can be flavored by the addition of the diced leaves of those species having a sour taste.

SORREL SOUP
Wash about a handful of sorrel and put in a pan with a little water (not covered). Cook slowly for 30 minutes. Put 4 cups of milk with a small whole white onion in a double boiler. Add 2 teaspoons of butter and 2 tablespoons of flour (blended to avoid lumps) to the hot milk. Let stand, add sorrel and strain. Season to taste. This serves about 6 people.

The tender leaves have been eaten raw in salads. Many people in this area have used the seed as a substitute for tobacco or in a mixture with it; in fact, the docks are often called "Indian tobacco." We have tried it and it does seem to be a reasonably good substitute. In addition the Indians gathered the ripe seeds of the docks and ground them into a meal that they used to make bread and mush.

The species are abundant, the leaves are bulky and palatable, making them an excellent survival source. The usually brown conspicuous, seedlike fruits of some kinds may protrude above a snow cover, and not only provide food for winter birds but are also available as food for some hungry human being.

Species:
About 25 species have been listed for the West, many of them famous food producers, but a few we found rather unpleasant tasting, although, none ever caused actual illness. The most of them we really enjoyed.

Portulaca spp.
PURSLANE, PORTULACA

Description:

Annual plants with rather fleshy, succulent stems and leaves; stems usually prostrate or sprawling, up to 1 foot long or more; leaves flattened but still thickish, small; petals about ⅛ inch long, yellow or sometimes copper-colored to purple; fruits up to ½ inch long; seeds very small.

Waste places, fields and gardens, often as a weed but sometimes well away from cultivated areas. Widespread in the United States. (*P. oleracea* is the common purslane.) In our area usually at low to medium elevations.

Use:

These are fleshy plants well known to gardeners as weeds that are hard to dry out and kill once they are pulled up. They have been widely used as food, and forms of them are actually cultivated in several parts of the world. The young shoots are used raw as a salad, often mixed with other plants because of the somewhat sour taste. We were once served a mixed salad at a restaurant in this area, and found that it contained leaves of the common purslane, but this may have been accidental! Because of the high water content (listed by Storer at 92.61 percent), they can be eaten raw to quench the thirst. The succulent young stems and leaves can be pickled in vinegar and sugar, following any pickle recipe.

Common purslane has long been a favorite when used for greens. The seeds have a way of germinating following summer rains, so that young growth may be available continuously up to late fall. Also, a single patch can be harvested all summer by picking off the young shoots as needed, and allowing the new ones to grow out for future use. We selected young plants, washed them, removed the roots, and boiled them for about 15 minutes (at 5,000 feet), sometimes changing the water

COMMON PURSLANE (*Portulaca oleracea*)

once. We have tried them in the ways that one would cook spinach, and found them to be excellent. They have a rather mild taste with a somewhat mucilaginous texture but this does not detract from their pleasant, slightly sour flavor. If the fatty feeling bothers you, try mixing the greens with those from other plants such as mustard. Some have suggested disguising this slippery texture by mixing the purslane shoots with bread crumbs and beaten eggs, baking the mixture in the oven until done. Because of their mucilaginous quality, the young stems have long been popular for thickening soup.

The Indians and Mexicans at one time dried large quantities of this plant by spreading the young stems out in the hot sun on the roofs. This dried material was found by Storer to be fairly high in albuminoids (30.25%) and carbohydrates (34.73%). It could then be soaked up later and boiled as a potherb.

The seeds of purslane, although very small, have been used as food, particularly by the Indians. A pile of these plants in fruiting condition can be placed on a flat rock or canvas and left to dry in the sun. Or they can be placed in a sack of paper or cloth to dry. In any case, the seeds will fall to the bottom, can be gathered, winnowed or sifted, and ground into a meal or flour. These seeds can be used in various ways, but we thought them rather tasteless when tried by themselves.

These are excellent salad plants or potherbs, often available in quantities, and are relatively easy to identify. Since they sometimes grow abundantly in isolated areas they may have value as an emergency food.

Species:

About 6 species have been recorded for the West, mostly from Arizona, but the common purslane (*P. oleracea*—the species illustrated), is the only one that is widely distributed.

Chenopodium spp.
LAMBS QUARTERS, PITSEED GOOSEFOOT, PIGWEED

A rather variable group of plants. The following treatment is limited to the common *C. album* and *C. berlandieri* and their close relatives. Some botanists hold that the two should be merged into one species.

Description:

Annual or perennial plants, whitish-green in color as if the leaves and stems were sprinkled with small flakes of white powder; stems 1-4 feet tall; leaves often broadly arrow-shaped; flowers very inconspicuous, lacking petals; fruit small and one-seeded, borne in clusters, often many to a plant.

Waste ground and fields, often a common weed. Widely distributed over the United States.

Use:

The seeds were commonly used by the Indians as a source of meal for bread or gruel. They can be gathered in large quantities in various ways; for example, by placing them in large paper or cloth sacks, or by beating them out on rocks or canvas. The seeds are small and smooth so it may be necessary to boil them, mash them, and then dry the material before grinding. The flour is dark colored from the blackish seed coats, but bakes up into a nice tasting and surely a nutritious product. Some people describe the taste as somewhat "mousey" or "weedy" but pleasant withal. The seeds can be parched and eaten partly raw, but the taste may not be to your liking, and we have found that the seeds are so small they are hard to chew.

The young leaves and tender shoots have long been used in salads. However, the plant is most popular as a potherb cooked and served like spinach. It is one of our favorites and we find very few people who do not enjoy it, once they have

PIGWEED (*Chenopodium berlandieri*)

overcome any prejudice they may have of eating "weeds." They cook down surprisingly in bulk, so gather plenty of material and use only the young growth. Boil them a bit longer than spinach, say 30-40 minutes (or 5 minutes at 15 lbs. pressure in a cooker). Several writers advise changing the water once, but we have never found this necessary. You can find this out for yourself by experimentation.

Species:

Over 20 species of *Chenopodium* have been listed for the West. They vary greatly in general appearance, some having very narrow leaves and others very broad ones. A few species have their parts spotted with small resin dots or sticky hairs that give them a rank unpleasant taste and odor. A strong aromatic tea has been brewed from them but they will automatically be avoided by most of us.

Viola spp.
VIOLET

Description:

Perennial plants; stems varying from very short to rather long (as is here pictured); leaves rather variable in shape but commonly narrow to broadly heart-shaped, the latter shape most common; flowers solitary on short or long stalks, varying in color from yellow, white, pink, rose to the characteristic violet-purple, with a short spur or sac at the base (but inconspicuous non-showy ones often borne later on, at or below the ground); fruit a podlike dry capsule opening along 3 lines.

The violets grow in a variety of habitats. A few like rocky open places but the most of them seem to prefer shade and moist soil.

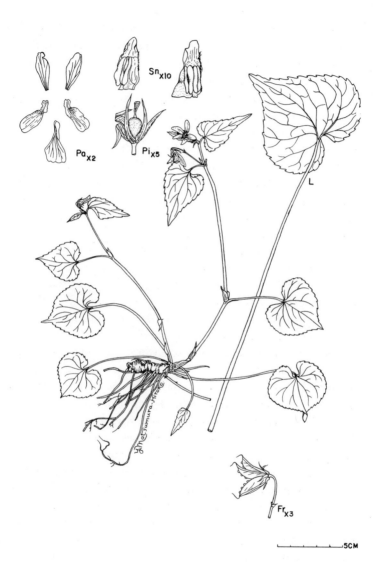

Sn x10

Pa x2

Pi x5

L

Fr x3

5CM

VIOLET *(Viola canadensis)*

Use:

Apparently all species of violets are edible, even the garden
varieties. We have tried about ten native species and found
them all good, with no objectionable flavor or harsh bitterness
in any of them. It has been said that violets are cultivated for
food in the gardens in Europe and we know of a few people
in this area who raise them for salads. The young leaves and
flower buds are used raw. The favorite mixture of ours con-
sists of head lettuce, halved cherry tomatoes, peeled fresh
carrots, shredded violet leaves and other native salad plants
as available. A few drops of vinegar can be used as a dressing.
The leaves and buds are best in the spring, but even in late
summer young leaves can be selected that will make an acceptable salad. We have found the raw violet leaves tender and
good but perhaps just a bit flat tasting when eaten alone.

The leaves and flowers can be boiled to make an acceptable
potherb. Again we like to use them mixed with other plants
of more pronounced taste. Violets are often used to thicken
soup, especially in the southern part of the United States
where they may be called "wild okra."

The flowers can be candied like rose petals and are for sale
in certain stores of the area. They have also been used to give
a flavor to vinegar. The latter procedure is very simple. The
flowers are crammed into a bottle, as many as can be con-
veniently forced in, then white wine vinegar is added. This
is corked and allowed to stand for about 4 weeks. Then the
vinegar is strained and used as "violet vinegar."

The violet leaves make a good substitute for tea. In fact,
many of the old timers in this area fondly recall that they
drank delicious violet-leaf tea when they were children. Long
boiling does not make the tea bitter, and a little added sugar
improves the taste to us. Violet-leaf tea is for sale in a few
food stores of this area.

Species:

Over 20 species have been recorded from the West. The one illustrated (*V. canadensis*) is rather widely distributed. It has flowers varying from whitish to light purple.

CHAPTER III: FRUITS, SEEDS AND MISCELLANEOUS (like Apple, Wheat and Tea)

THIS CHAPTER is concerned with the use of wild plants as fleshy fruits, dry seedlike fruits, seeds, and as a host of miscellaneous products like tea, fibers, smoking material, soap, etc.

Fleshy fruits are rather conspicuous and are often brightly colored; this makes them rather easy to locate in the fields and forests. They seem to be the commonest food that is avidly seized upon by people lost in the wilderness, at least to judge by occasional newspaper accounts. Eating such fruits does create a certain problem in identification, for when they are ripe the characteristic flowers that preceded them have usually faded away. Of course, most fruits are definitely characteristic in themselves, and easy to recognize once you become familiar with them. Many of them are closely related to commonly cultivated ones like raspberry and strawberry. Fortunately, only a few berries in our area are seriously poisonous. One of the suspected ones is the baneberry (*Actaea*), which has attractive shining red or white fruits, another well known one is poison ivy (*Rhus*) with waxy white berries. The best way to proceed is to learn these poisonous plants in all their growth phases, and avoid their fruits entirely. Then you can eat, with reasonable safety, any other palatable berry in the area. A fairly safe general rule would be to avoid all red or white fruits, sticking to the blue or black colored ones, but then you would miss out on some very delicious ones like those of the wild strawberry.

Some people have suggested that such fruits be selected from your memory of the appearance of their cultivated counterparts. This could certainly be done with some like strawberries, a fruit with which everyone is familiar. That is one reason a few common ones like wild strawberry, wild grape and wild plum are omitted from this treatment. Everyone surely knows them. Such a procedure will not solve the whole problem anyway as some real good fleshy fruits like the rose and serviceberry have nothing resembling them in the market. But a visit to some extensive fruit store might be of value to anyone before sampling the wild types.

Fleshy fruits are often very seasonable, lasting but a short time. Trying to gather them often turns out to be a race with the birds. However, some fleshy fruits do remain on the twigs even into the winter and may be handy to gather, especially in times of emergency. Such a fruit would be that of the wild rose (*Rosa*). These fruits become dry and withered, but can be softened in the mouth or in water, and they seem to us to provide some taste and nutrition, even when a layer of snow is on the ground.

Such fleshy fruits are relatively high in water content, and under certain arid conditions this characteristic could be a life saver. They may be relatively low in actual number of calories, but do have the reputation of being high in essential vitamins. Usually, one of your recipes for cultivated fruits will do equally well for the most of the wild ones, especially if the two plants are somewhat related. If you wish to make jam or jelly from wild berries, it is wise to try a small amount first to see if the addition of pectin is necessary.

Fleshy fruits are sometimes locally abundant, but are hard to store, at least under primitive conditions. Under survival conditions it would be wise to avoid gorging too heavily on them; consider drying a portion of them in the sun for future use. The Indians prepared their famous pemmican using various native berries. This was made in several ways, but the fleshy fruits were commonly mixed with dried lean meat which had been pounded to a powderlike consistency. Then melted fat was poured over the mixture and allowed to solidify. The product may not sound very appetizing to many of us, but this concentrated food played an important part in the exploration and settlement of the wilderness, especially in the North.

One thing can be said for eating wild, fleshy fruits. Most of them have a tangy and delicious taste; this is usually much more pronounced than that of their cultivated counterparts. If you do try them extensively you are in for some new and different taste sensations.

The dry fruits and seeds of native edible plants are of special value as food, since they are relatively high in nutritive value as compared with most other plant parts. It must be admitted that many of them are very small. This creates a problem in gathering them in quantities, but, on the other hand, they are often borne in large numbers on one individual. If you secure a mature plant when these structures are about ready to be shed naturally, and then shake or beat the plant over a cloth or flat rock surface, you will probably be surprised by the amount of your harvest. Many of us have learned to collect these parts bearing the fruits or seeds just before they are ready to shed, and then stow them away in large cloth or paper sacks to dry out. Later on these sacks can be shaken or beaten and the harvest collected in the bottom. The leaf pieces and dry bracts can be removed by winnowing in the breeze, or by using a sieve.

Dry seeds and fruits are better if ground up, especially if they are very small. If you are under primitive conditions a couple of stones of proper shape (mano and metate) can be used. Such cracked or ground material can be utilized in many ways. In many cases the enclosing bracts and coverings can be ground up right along with the contents. If the seeds or fruits are ground fine enough a kind of flour can be secured.

Of course, plants with these parts infected with disease (such as ergot or smut) should be avoided, but these blackish malformations can be readily recognized. Seeds and dry fruits store for long periods of time, and are fairly easily carried around from place to place. This may be necessary under certain types of emergency conditions. Fortunately, very few of our native plants produce poisonous seeds or dry fruits, but of course it would be wise to avoid those from known poisonous species. If you have the patience you can secure a large amount of food material from the dry fruits and seeds of native plants, and many of them will also provide you with new, agreeable taste sensations.

Many plants can be used as a substitute for commercial tea. It is surprising the number of species that have been used to brew beverages; you may wish to experiment a bit yourself. Avoid known poisonous plants, of course. The part used should be dried quickly in the shade, then stored in tight containers for future use. The young leaves or fresh flowers should be selected, if these are to be the parts to be used. The general rule for making "tea" is to use $\frac{1}{2}$ to 1 teaspoon of the dried material to a cup of boiling water. If fresh material is used it will take about twice as much. Otherwise, use about the same procedure as you would in brewing commercial tea. Some of us enjoy mixing the product of several plants, often adding a little commercial tea. These substitutes make a more or less agreeable hot drink, but it must be admitted that they may lack, for you, the stimulating quality of the original tea. Some grocery store owners take pride in stocking a wide variety of unusual tea substitutes.

This chapter was the hardest one to pare down to the planned size. The number of possible plants we could mention is legion, and it is too bad that so few can be included here. The use of such plants is often more casual than critical, so the real, important food-producing ones have to take precedent.

Quercus spp.
OAK

Description:

Shrubs or trees; leaves varying from unlobed to shallowly or deeply lobed in from the sides (the one illustrated shows the typical lobed leaves); pollen producing flowers (staminate) in drooping catkins; fruit a characteristic acorn, nutlike, borne in a basal cup.

The various species of oaks are widespread in the United States. Some have evergreen, others deciduous leaves, these lobed or unlobed. Naturally they are very diverse in general appearance but all bear the well known "acorn."

Use:

The oak species of the West are variable, inclined to intergrade, and we have suspected that they are not very well understood by botanists. They are often divided into two groups, the white oaks and the black oaks (including red oaks). These differ in several respects, but the black oaks characteristically have at least some of the leaf veins protruding from the margins or apexes as short weak bristles while this is not the case in the white oaks. In general the white-oak acorns are preferred as food because they are less bitter tasting and it is fortunate that our common oaks often belong to this group.

Acorns have often been used all over the world where oaks grow, and in many places furnished the main source of nourishment for certain Indian tribes. The bitter astringent taste is thought to be caused at least in part by tannin, but fortunately this can be readily removed. The Indians gathered the acorns and cracked off the outer shell, sometimes boiling or roasting the nuts first to facilitate this operation. The kernels were often ground into a meal, and could then be leached with water in various ways to remove any possible bitter taste. The simplest

OAK *(Quercus gambelii)*

method was to place the meal in a very fine mesh basket or bag, and immerse it in a stream for several hours to several days. This meal was used alone to make mush, thicken soup, make bread or pancakes, or in combination with cornmeal.

Sometimes wood ashes were used to provide a kind of lye and this was used in the leaching process. This leaching often took place in holes made in sand or gravel along a stream. The dough contaminated with sand was often used in making soup; the sand grains were supposed to sink to the bottom of the container. The ground up acorn, or possibly the shells only, were often roasted, ground and used in making a beverage that was used as a substitute for coffee. The ground up kernels were sometimes boiled in water and the oil allowed to rise to the surface. This oil was skimmed off and used in various ways. Meriam once analyzed acorn meal and found about 20-25% fat present. The protein was about 4.5 to 5.5% and the carbohydrates around 60%. It would accordingly appear that acorn meal is a reasonably nourishing food product. The leaching process did not seem to remove very much of the essential food elements.

The different kinds of oaks not only vary a good deal in bitterness, but different individual plants of the same species differ somewhat in this respect. We have collected acorns that could actually be eaten raw, but even these had a faint suggestion of a bitter aftertaste. We have boiled the whole or broken kernels in water for 45 minutes, changing the water several times. The discarded water turned yellow in color and apparently carried away the tannin, because the finished kernels were pleasant tasting. These kernels were then ground into a meal. However, the raw kernels can also be ground into a similar meal if you do not mind a slight suggestion of bitterness. Maybe this will actually taste good to you. To us, the flour was excellent, gave breads a crunchy texture and an added flavor. A mixture of half acorn flour and half wheat flour made very acceptable pancakes. Here is a general recipe that sounds practical for making bread: use 2 cups acorn meal combined with 2 cups cornmeal and 8 cups wheat flour. Cracked acorn kernels can also be used as nuts to flavor cookies and cakes; to us they taste much like other nuts.

Some years the acorn crop is scarce and only certain clumps of oaks produce much of a yield. Since you have to run a race with birds and animals they may best be collected just as they ripen. They should be shelled at once, as many are infected with a wormlike larvae that can spoil all or the most of your stored material. The kernels can be dried raw or first leached in the ways described, and then dried, in which form they keep at least for several months. We have found these dried kernels can be placed in the mouth, allowed to soak up for several minutes, and when chewed provide a palatable mouthful. This could be of value in certain emergency situations.

The acorn, when properly used, provides what we have voted to be one of the most palatable wild foods. It is often produced in abundance, is easily harvested, the individual kernel is large and easily processed. The astringent taste of many kinds is somewhat of a drawback, but this can be overcome as indicated by repeated boilings or leaching in cold water. The Indians used their common method of mixing certain clay soil with the meal to hide this taste. Fernald and Kinsey suggested a nicer sounding method; they just added a small amount of powdered gelatine to the acorn meal which helped to remove the bitter taste.

The oaks in our area do sometimes cause poisoning to livestock which have grazed the foliage but there is no suggestion that the poisonous substance is in the acorn. We know of no record of human beings being poisoned by eating the fruit of oaks.

Species:

About 16 species of oaks have been reported from the West, the most of them from the southern part. Species resembling the one illustrated (*Q. gambelii* or close relatives), seem to be most widely distributed.

5CM

COLORADO PIÑON PINE (*Pinus edulis*)

Pinus spp.
PINE

Description:
   Short to tall trees; needles evergreen, usually borne 2 to 5
in clusters but rarely single; bearing woody-scaled cones; seeds
borne on the scales, from small and winged to wingless and up
to ½ inch long. The kinds having large wingless seeds are the
ones most utilized and are often called "piñon pines."

Foothills, mesas, canyon and rocky slopes. Species of the genus widespread from low elevations up to timberline.

The large seeded species mentioned are the ones particularly discussed here.

Use:

The seeds of piñon pine were at one time an important food source to the Indians, and are still gathered and sold by various groups. One sees the nuts for sale in many grocery stores of the area, and they are often exported to other localities where they are utilized in various ways, often in making candy. New York City used to take the bulk of the export nuts. Some years we have a small crop and the surest way to secure the seeds is to gather the unopened cones, put them in a safe place to dry, and then gather the shattered nuts later on from the dried cones. The Indians expected a bumper crop every seven years, which was followed, they thought, by an epidemic of smallpox. This could well be the case as during such a harvest there naturally would be an intermingling of various groups, apparently even of enemy factions, which could aid in spreading possible infection.

The nuts were harvested in the fall or possibly in the early winter when the cones were opening and the seeds were about ready to fall. Canvas was spread on the ground and the tree was shaken to bring down the seeds. The ones on the trees were often collected in bags by climbers. If the cones were not open they were roasted until the scales separated. Rat's nests were often raided. These were found in rock crevices, in hollow logs or under heaps of twigs, one nest often yielding up to 30 lbs. of seed.

Some of the seeds are aborted, with only an empty shell remaining. The flotation method is sometimes used to separate the good ones from the bad. However, from our own experience we have found that some good seeds will float on water. The seeds can be eaten raw at once, or stored for the winter. They have a pleasant oil-nutty taste, and have a nutritive value that has been listed as follows: Protein, 14.6%; fat 61.9%; carbohydrates, 17.3%; ash, 2.8%; with a fuel value per pound of 3,205 calories.

The raw seeds become rancid after a time, the Indians say after one year, so they were usually roasted before storing. In any event, this roasting cracked or weakened the seed coat. They were then cracked between rocks, and the hulls winnowed out if this was considered necessary. Apparently at least a few hulls were considered by some tribes to improve the final flavor. In any case, the contents were ground into a meal, and used in gruel, to thicken soup, to make cakes, or in various other ways. The meal was also used to make a kind of pudding, often mixed with pulp of yucca fruits, or used as a substitute for peanut butter. Often it was mixed with cornmeal or meal from sunflower seeds.

Cracking the shells of raw or roasted piñon nuts between the teeth, separating out the kernels with the tongue and enjoying their sweet nutty flavor is an experience everyone should have. It isn't over right away; a bag of piñon nuts lasts a long while. You can even get them from vending machines some places as you would salted peanuts. A nickel used to buy a fair sized handful.

The needles of this pine can yield a satisfactory tea by boiling them. This has to be done carefully to control the strength desired. All pines probably make an acceptable beverage, but the Boy Scouts of our acquaintance seem to prefer tea made from ponderosa pine (*Pinus ponderosa*).

The inner bark of piñon pine and also other species was used as a starvation food by the Indians and early white people. The south side of the trunk was usually used, and the outer bark removed in the spring. Then the more tender, fleshy, mucilaginous layer between the bark and the wood was scraped or peeled off. According to report, some people even enjoy the taste of this raw. We tried it from ponderosa pine (*Pinus ponderosa*) in May and voted it flat, resinous tasting, slightly fibrous, and rather leathery. This inner bark can be cooked or dried for storage, later to be cooked or ground into a meal. We doubt if it will be a popular item except in emergencies.

Species:

About 20 species of pines have been reported for the West and the seeds of all are edible. However, only 2 or 3 have large seeds that have become famous as food. The species illustrated (*P. edulis*) is widely distributed especially in the middle and southern parts of the West.

Rosa spp.
ROSE

Description:

Shrubs with upright or sprawling stems, these bearing prickles and sometimes bristles also; leaves always of 3 or more divisions (leaflets); flowers large and showy, our native species colored some shade of rose, but this often fading to whitish; fruit rather fleshy, somewhat like an apple, the fruit often called a "hip," red or orange-red in color, made up of a vase-shaped, fleshy covering, this lined on the inside with several to many bony, seedlike structures.

Woods, plains, thickets and hills. Widespread over North America. In our area usually found below 10,000 feet elevation.

Use:

The rose species seem to be difficult for botanists to classify, and certainly the fruits are very variable. Sometimes they will

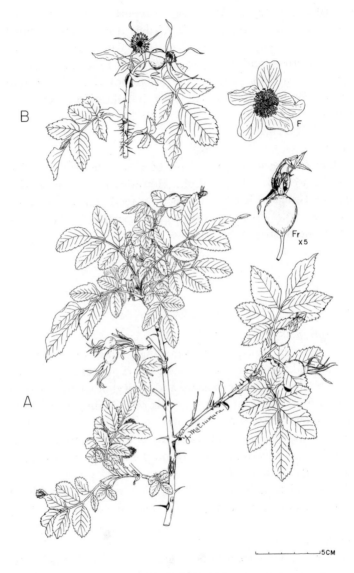

5CM

ROSE (*Rosa* spp.)

be large, up to 1 inch or more wide, with a relatively thick pulpy layer; sometimes they are small and less fleshy; often both kinds are present in different areas on what botanists may call plants of the same species. The bony, seedlike structures in the center are more or less hairy and these hairs are rather a nuisance. We have found a good deal of variation in the flavor of rose hips collected at different places and at different elevations. When you locate a desirable fruit-producing area, it is wise to remember it and go back to it the next year.

Various parts of the rose plant are used in many ways by people all over the world, but the fleshy fruits are the most widely utilized. Makino, in his *Illustrated Flora of Japan,* mentioned that *Rosa rugosa* hips are rather fleshy and are used as food in Japan, particularly by children. Rose fruits are listed as high in vitamins A and C, particularly the latter, and are noted for their antiscorbutic effects. In World War II they were collected in quantity in Europe particularly in England and the Scandinavian countries. In 1943 about five hundred tons of rose hips were collected in Great Britain and made into a syrup called National Rose Hip Syrup according to Hill. We have recently purchased rose-hip powder in a local grocery store. It had been processed and packaged in Sweden and exported to this country to be used for flavoring and for soups, according to the label. Pills made from the fruits have been offered for sale as a source of vitamin C.

The fruits should be taken when ripe, some say after frost. We have found that a bright red color does not necessarily indicate that the fruit is really ripe. If the fruits are of any size at all, they can be split longitudinally and the inner seedlike structures removed. This gets rid of the hairs that are attached to them. The blossom end is usually removed and the pulp can be eaten raw or stewed, or can be used to make wine, jam or jelly. We used the "mayhaw" recipe given in the Sure-Jell directions and no trouble was experienced in getting the juice to jell. The color was a dark, rich red and the taste was very good, not too strong but not too bland. The only drawback we found was the time and labor expended in securing and processing a large amount of the fruits. A blend of rose juice with that of other more easily secured fruits like apple, should be tried. We made a puree following the recipe given by Angier.

Rose Hip Puree

Grind 4 cups of rose hips. Add 2½ cups of water and boil 20 minutes in a covered, enameled saucepan. Then rub through a sieve. This can be bottled in small glass containers and heated for 20 minutes in boiling water. Angier suggested using it to flavor soups or mixed with tapioca pudding. We have used the puree with stewed meats, with vegetables such as Zucchini squash, green beans, and in soups, adding it just before serving so as not to cook out the vitamins. We did not care for it alone but found it quite acceptable as a flavor.

The rose hips can be dried and kept for long periods. These dried fruits can be ground into a powder, even leaving the seedlike structures in if the fruits are small. This powder can be used to flavor various kinds of other foods and drinks. We added it to pancakes, concluding that it blended in well but did not add much to the flavor.

Even the green fruits, when peeled and cooked, have been utilized as food. The young shoots in the spring are said to make an acceptable potherb. The leaves have been used to make a tea. The rose petals can be eaten raw, in salads, candied, used in making syrup, or dried and made into a bevarage like tea. The rose roots were used likewise by certain of the Indians for tea making, and the inner bark was sometimes smoked like tobacco. The petals are often dried and placed in jars to be used as a perfume or have actually been used to give an odor and flavor to butter.

Rose hips dry on the twigs and can be used for at least the early part of the winter. They may protrude above the snow and furnish the only readily available nourishment for hungry wayfarers. We have often collected a handful of these dried fruits and let them soak in the mouth, after which they were chewed on with some satisfaction. We consider rose hips an excellent emergency food, both raw and cooked, as well as a fairly good source of general food. How strange that so many of our parents have warned us as children that these red fruits are poisonous. Even the Indians had some such mistaken idea for several members of the Ute Tribe told us that if we should touch rose hips we would itch all over, the information apparently handed down by their parents, not from personal experience.

Species:

About 8 species of roses are listed for the area. They all are similar in appearance (like the illustration), and all have edible fruits.

Yucca spp.
YUCCA, SPANISH BAYONET, SOAPWEED

Description:

Plants perennial; stems from short to elongated and woody, even sometimes forming a definite tree; leaves crowded, narrow and stiff, sharp-pointed, margins usually lacking teeth but typically bearing short fibers as illustrated; flowers in clusters, the flower stalk arising from the leaf cluster, often large; flowers very large, often over 4 inches long, white, greenish-white to cream-colored; fruit becoming dry and splitting open at maturity or fleshy and remaining closed.

CFr

Fi

In

F2

5CM

Yucca (*Yucca baccata*)

SPANISH BAYONET *(Yucca glauca)*

Dry plains, slope and desert places. Abundant in the south-ern part of the West.

The yuccas form two groups depending on the type of fruit formed. Each group is discussed separately below.

Use:

A. *Fleshy fruits* (see illustration of *Y. baccata*—the datil yucca)

These were important economic plants to the Indians of the Southwest, who found them useful in several ways. The species of *Yucca* in general can be separated into two groups as men-tioned, based on the characters of the fruit. In one group the fruits are dry when ripe, separating into sections and allowing the seeds to fall out. In the second group the fruits become fleshy, somewhat on the order of an apple or a banana; in such a case the seeds do not fall out in any definite fashion, but are freed when the pulp decays away. The fruits of datil yucca are fleshy at maturity, and have often provided a source of a sweet, palatable, succulent food in an area where other such fruits may be few and far between.

The Indians split the fruits open, then the seeds and fibers were scraped out. Sometimes they were roasted or boiled be-fore opening, sometimes the outer peels were removed but often they were left on. The fleshy pulp was used in various ways, for example, as a filling for a pie. The Indians dried this pulp for later use by cutting it in strips and hanging it out in the sun. Sometimes the fruit was baked, the skins and seeds removed, and the fleshy part boiled down to a paste. This was molded into cakes and dried. Often the cakes were perforated by a sharp stick to facilitate rapid drying. These cakes could be later boiled and used in such things as gruel, dumplings, bread, conserve, etc.

The flowers of the datil yucca are usually abundant every year, but abundant fruit may not develop each season. The pollination system is almost unbelievable, involving a small white yucca moth that often stays throughout the day in the closed flowers. In the night time the moth carries pollen from flower to flower, forcing it on the proper receptacle (stigma) in a most deliberate looking fashion. In any event, the system apparently does not operate very effectively every year. The fruits are reported to be cathartic to some degree, particularly to those not accustomed to them, so it would be best to be somewhat moderate in eating them, at least at first. The large black seeds were roasted by the Indians and eaten whole, or were ground into a kind of meal. Partly mature fruit can be used, or these can be ripened after picking, like bananas. In fact, the Indians often gathered them before ripening in order to circumvent the animals and birds who also appreciated this desert delicacy.

The flowers of all the yuccas we have encountered are edible but the datil yucca does not rate very high in this respect according to reports and our own experience. We have boiled them and found them rather bitter and "soapy" tasting. Perhaps a change or two of water in the process would help. The Indians reported that the older flowers were the best. The young tender flower stalks can be cut out just as they are emerging from their cluster of leaves and prepared like mescal or agave (see *Agave*).

In addition, the fibers in the leaves or the actual leaves themselves were much used by the Indians for such things as sandals, leggings, mats, cord, rope, baskets, etc. To obtain the fibers they would soak the leaves in water until they became soft, then pound out the fibers with a mallet. Finally, the roots can be crushed to provide a fairly good substitute for soap. Simply mash the root portions in water and agitate the liquid to a lather. We know of several people who have used this datil as soap and consider it especially good for washing the hair. Yucca soap made from this plant was on the market before 1899, made by a soap company in Illinois. Certainly this is a valuable plant for general use and especially useful in an emergency.

B. *Dry fruits* (see the illustration of *Y. glauca*).

The immature or partly developed fruit of these types are edible, and were once very popular with the Indians. We boiled them for 15 to 25 minutes, then sliced them and served them with butter, salt and pepper. The taste reminded us of summer squash, slightly sweet, but with a lingering background of bitterness. We have found that the most of this bitter taste can be removed by peeling the fruit before cooking. We have also baked the young fruits for 20 minutes at 300 degrees F. wrapped in aluminum foil. They were then sliced, buttered and seasoned. The taste was somewhat bitter, but not obnoxiously so. The Indians used to bake them in the ashes of a fire; this method would be worth remembering, especially in an emergency. The pods can be sliced raw or after cooking, then dried in the sun for future use, the way the Indians did it. If the fruits are past their prime you may have to remove the seeds before you eat them, but the young pods can be eaten seeds and all. The Indian method of digging a fireless cooker (see *Agave*), can be used to prepare the fruit and also the young flower stalk. The latter is cut off just as it emerges from the leaf cluster, then cooked, and the whitish inner portion eaten.

The flowers of this and related species of yucca are eaten raw as a salad or boiled to make a potherb. Standley said that in 1920 it was common to find yucca flowers for sale in the food markets of Mexico. We boiled the flowers for about 15-25 minutes, serving them with seasoning, vinegar or butter. They were very pleasant tasting to us, and certainly could be prepared in various special ways as you would spinach or asparagus.

The yucca leaves can be tied into bundles to make a primitive kind of broom, or used to make sandals, matting, etc. The leaves can be soaked in water until soft and the fibers can then be beaten out with a wooden mallet. These fibers can then be woven into cord or rope.

Finally, the roots of this yucca can be used like the other species as a substitute for soap. We dug out pieces of the root, scraped them in a basin in warm water and agitated them to form a lather; this was not very copious, but still moderately so. We would say on the basis of our experience that it was about the quality of rather poor soap, of course much cheaper and sometimes more available. Yucca soap has been marketed at various times in the past, but has never become very popular although some people like it to wash the hair. If you try this soap from yucca roots, perhaps you will agree with the Indians who claimed "It makes the hair grow."

It can be seen that the dry-fruited yuccas may be useful in several ways, both generally and in time of emergency. It should be pointed out that the yucca leaves contain salicylic acid and the roots saponin, and should never be eaten. In fact, it would be wise to eat any part of this yucca with some moderation until you are sure it has no bad effect on you; although we have never noticed any of this on ourselves. If the flowers or the young fruits are used as food they should be looked over carefully for insect adults or larvae, especially if you are one of those people who prefer to keep animal and vegetable foods separate on your plate!

Species:

Around 15 different species of yucca have been reported from our area, the most of them from southern New Mexico and Arizona. They vary greatly in general habit, from the almost stemless types (like the ones illustrated), to treelike ones like the "Joshua Tree" (*Y. brevifolia*) of the Southwest.

Prosopis spp.
Mesquite, Screwbean, Honey Mesquite

Description:

Shrubs or small trees; leaves rather fernlike, the smallest divisions (leaflets) up to 1 inch long; flowers in narrow spikes up to 3 inches long; flowers small, greenish-yellow; pods of 2 kinds, either straight or nearly so (as in the illustrated honey mesquite), or else twisted into a tight, narrow, straight spiral (as in the screwbean), neither splitting open when ripe.

Plains, washes and bottom lands along streams. Scattered over the southern part of the West area, often abundant locally.

Use:

The honey mesquite (*P. juliflora*—see illustration), at one time was an important food producer for the Indians of the Southwest, and the fruits are still used by them. The ripe pods contain numerous seeds, between which is a considerable quantity of yellowish, mealy substance that is sweet and agreeable to the taste. These pods were pounded or ground into a kind of meal, some of the seeds and coarse parts of the pods were picked out, and the resulting product used as food in various ways. For example, it might be mixed with water and eaten at once, or allowed to ferment for a time, eventually even producing a kind of beer. The meal was often moistened, made into cakes which were baked in the sun, and stored for future use.

The dry pods could be stored in baskets or granaries of various kinds, sometimes in pits rimmed with circular stones. These ancient structures can still be seen in various parts of the Southwest. The fruits were ground as needed, as they were said to keep in good condition until the next year's crop.

The isolated seeds were also pulverized into a meal, or cooked with other food products. They are said to have a

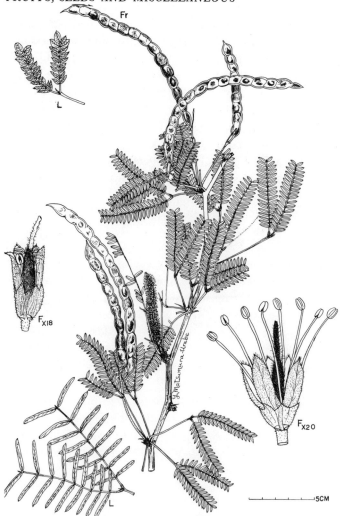

HONEY MESQUITE (*Prosopis juliflora*)

pleasant lemon flavor. The pods and seeds consist of about $\frac{1}{3}$ sugar and the meal from them is thought to be highly nutritious.

Hungry travelers can chew on the ripe, raw pods and secure at least some nutrition. The mingled acidity and sweetness may also help to quench the thirst. The macerated pods would certainly constitute a good emergency food. For example, the ground up mixture can be soaked in water or cooked in water, the liquid can then be drunk with as much of the solid material as possible. One drawback is that the pods and seeds are commonly infected by a weevil and one might find oneself consuming a mixed animal and vegetable diet. This did not seem to bother the Indians much and probably wouldn't make much difference to any starving person.

The flowers have been eaten, stripping the flowers from their central stalk by drawing them between the teeth; they are reported to be sweet to the taste. As the name suggests, honey mesquite flowers are well known as a source of nectar for bees, and the plant is considered by some people to be the most important honey producing supply in the areas where it is abundant. A resinous secretion often appears from the bark which contains sugar, and this is sometimes used for candy making. Certainly, this plant has been one of the area's most important food producing source, and could be very valuable in an emergency.

The "screwbean" (*Prosopis pubescens*) is a related plant, but differs in the fruit characters. These fruits, instead of being straight or merely curved, are twisted into a spiral, much like a corkscrew. These pods are used in much the same way as are those of honey mesquite.

Species:

Only the 2 species mentioned above, (*P. juliflora* & *P. pubescens*) are present in our area as native plants. Both are widely distributed.

Rubus, spp.

RASPBERRY, BLACKBERRY, THIMBLE-BERRY, SALMON BERRY,
BRAMBLE

Description:

Stems becoming woody, unarmed or bearing stiff bristles or
prickles; leaves either large or undivided (simple—*R. parviflorus* in the illustration), or divided into 3-5 segments (compound—like *R. strigosus* in the illustration); flowers medium
to rather large in size, the petals sometimes over 1 inch long,
usually white in color; fruit a typical raspberry or blackberry
(as in the grocery stores), made up of a cluster of spherical
individual fleshy structures (drupelets), usually red or black in
color.

Woods or open places. Widespread in the West, from low
elevations to timberline in the mountains.

Use:

The fruit of the raspberries is composed of many fleshy
drupelets clustered together; when ripe these separate from
the hemispherical structure to which they were attached. The
blackberry fruit is similar, but the fleshy bodies, instead of falling away from their attachment structure, come away with it.
The recipes and suggestions given for raspberries will apply
equally well for blackberries. The common red raspberry produces a favorite fruit wherever it is found in any abundance,
and is preferred by many of us to the various cultivated forms.
It has a high tart flavor that is considered delicious by practically everyone; usually it is used to make jam, jelly and pies.
We have made the berries into jam following a standard recipe
for raspberries, but found the seeds were rather bothersome.
The product, however, was delicious, with a pleasing color,
taste and odor. We recommend that they be made into jelly

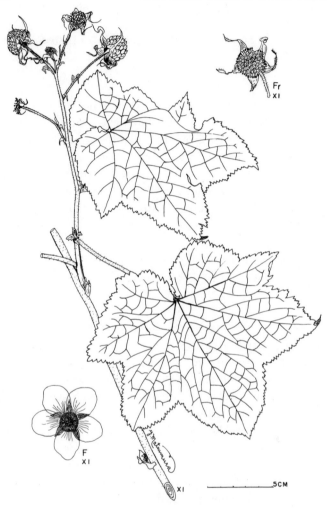

JAPANESE RASPBERRY (*Rubus parviflorus*)

instead, using the recipe on the jar or box of pectin. If the
fruit is somewhat unripe you may be able to get the product to
jell without this pectin, but it is better to play safe. Wild

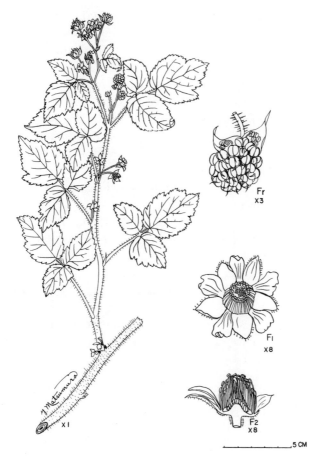

RED RASPBERRY (*Rubus strigosus*)

raspberry jelly is justly famous the country over. Another use is to mix the washed unsweetened fruit into vanilla or butterscotch instant pudding. This can be poured into a pie shell for an excellent quick raspberry cream pie.

In fact, any of your recipes for cultivated raspberries and blackberries can be used for the wild fruit. Many people of the area cultivate these plants in their gardens because they prefer them to the horticultural forms, but the plants are not ever-bearing, and have one main crop a year. The Indians ground up the fruit, dried it in the sun and were able to store it for later use, sometimes using it mixed with cornmeal. The young, tender, peeled shoots are edible, both raw and cooked like asparagus or spinach. A substitute for tea can be made from the leaves or the twigs, but it would be wise to take it slowly at first as some species may cause physiological trouble. Such "tea" appears for sale in a few of our local grocery stores. We have seen recipes for making soup and wine from raspberries that sound worth trying.

These are widespread, very useful plants under any conditions. The fruits become available over a period of several weeks, but in a good season a reasonable quantity can often be gathered at one time. We once directed a group of boys who were collecting seeds for a reseeding project. It was remarkable how few of the fruits found their way into the collecting sack, all of which suggests that the fruits taste excellent raw. They are available during their season as an emergency food.

Species:

We have at least 20 species of *Rubus* in our area (depending on who is counting). The common red raspberry is often called *R. idaeus* instead of *R. strigosus*.

Vaccinum spp.
WHORTLEBERRY, BLUEBERRY, GROUSEBERRY, BILBERRY, HUCKLEBERRY

Description:

Usually low shrubs, often less than 2 feet tall; leaves usually with small teeth on the margins; flowers white, greenish-yellow

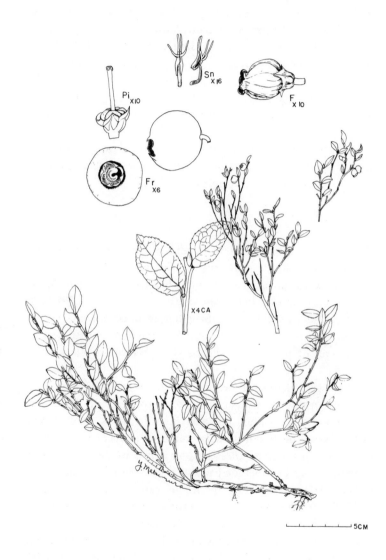

WHORTLEBERRY (*Vaccinium scoparium*)

to rose, rather small, often not over $\frac{1}{4}$ inch long, vase-shaped (like F of the illustration); fruit rather small, in most kinds less than $\frac{1}{2}$ inch long, a red, black or blue berry, which is crowned at the apex with the small withered remnants of the flowers.

Mountain slopes and valleys. Canada and the United States. Scattered over the West, especially in the northern part of the area.

Many common names have been applied to the different species. "Whortleberry" seems to be the one most used for the entire group and is accordingly used here.

Use:

This is a popular wild fruit, and in some areas where the larger fruited kinds grow the berries are gathered commercially. Our kinds often have small berries and may be stingy producers. One old-timer told us that they used to be much more abundant, but grazing sheep had thinned down the stand. You're right, he was a cattleman! We have had no trouble finding plenty of plants, but the berries were often few and far between.

The sweet, flavorful berries can be used in a variety of ways, eaten raw with sugar and cream, cooked into a sauce, or made into a pie. They are also favorite fruits to mix with various kinds of dough to make muffins, breads or pancakes; in fact, one can purchase these various mixes in the stores where whortleberries are included under the name of blueberries or huckleberries. They can be home canned, or the canned product can be bought at your grocery. Canned pie mixes are for sale, also a syrup made from this popular berry.

Whortle berries are famous for making jams and jellies, and are often mixed with other fruits like peaches or apples. We have used the following recipe.

Whortleberry Jam

4 cups crushed berries	1 package powdered pectin
2 tablespoons lemon juice	(such as Sure-Jell)

5 cups sugar

Mix berries, lemon juice, and pectin. Place over high heat and stir until it comes to a hard boil. Then add sugar and boil hard one minute. Remove from heat and alternately stir and skim for 5 minutes. Pour in scalded jelly glasses and seal with paraffin. It should make about 9 glasses. The black- or blue-fruited species in our area make a very good tasting jam with a brisk, pleasant flavor.

Pancakes made with these berries are usually available at any restaurant specializing in pancakes. If you make your own, then use any recipe mix for pancakes and stir in a cup of whortleberries. Boorman gave an interesting recipe which was called:

Canoe-Trip Pancakes

1 cup pancake or biscuit mix	Powdered milk (in proportion
1 powdered egg	to water)
1½ cups water	1 cup of whortleberries

Stir the pancake mix, the powdered milk and powdered egg together in a pan. Add water beating to a thin batter. Add berries. Makes about 12 small pancakes.

The Indians used to gather the berries and dry them in the sun or over the campfire. They were stored, and used later in various ways much as we do raisins. They used them to flavor other foods like meat, to thicken soup, or to work into their famous "pemmican" product. The berries dry fairly nicely, especially when finished off in an oven. It has been suggested that if the fresh fruit is sealed in a jar and placed in an ice box or refrigerator it will keep as long as a month. We have

never tried this, probably because we never had the will power
to keep such delicious fruit on hand for so long.

The leaves of whortleberry can be used fresh or dried to
make a kind of tea. Our experience has been that some kinds
make a pleasant tasting beverage, others not so good. (*Vaccinium myrtillus* is our favorite and appears for sale at one of
our local grocery stores). We have also been told that a wine
can be made from the fruit.

This is a very valuable group of fruit producing plants. The
species illustrated (*V. scoparium*) is widely distributed in the
West. Unfortunately, the small red fruits, although high in
flavor, are often stingily produced.

Species:

About 20 species of *Vaccinum* grow in the West, the most of
them from the northern part and Canada.

Amelanchier spp.
SERVICEBERRY, JUNEBERRY, SHADBLOW, SARVICEBERRY

Description:

Shrubs or small trees; leaves oval or nearly round with
toothed margins; flowers in clusters, longer than broad; petals
white, rather narrow, 1/4 to 1/2 inch long; fruit applelike but
small, one that is 1/2 inch in diameter is considered to be a
fairly large one, purple-red to black when ripe.

Stream banks, moist hillsides, in woods or open ground.
Scattered over the West. The plants are rather conspicuous
in flower.

Use:

The different kinds of service berries all have edible fruit,
but they vary in size of the product and the relative amount

SERVICEBERRY (*Amelanchier alnifolia*) ⊢————⊣ 5 CM

of pulp present. Even in the same species one can notice differences among races or even between individual trees. The amount of rainfall for the season or the moisture in the site where the plant grows affects this fruit size. The Indians used these fruits in large amounts. They can be eaten fresh, the only objectionable feature being the large seeds which may be bad tasting to some, but are said by some people to add to the flavor. The fruit can be dried and used as one would use raisins. They tend to dry on the plant and late in the season can be picked, eaten raw, or cooked into a puree or jam. Cooking makes the skins and seeds more palatable after this drying.

The Indians pounded the fruit, spread out the mass and let it dry in large cakes for future use. These cakes were used particularly to flavor stews and puddings, but they can be cooked by themselves. The serviceberry fruits were often used in making "pemmican," a discussion of which appears at the beginning of this chapter.

The fresh fruit can be used in any of the various ways that any fleshy fruit can be utilized. It makes good pies and may be canned for this purpose. Mrs. John May made an excellent jelly using the recipe on the package of Certo or Sure-Jell, substituting the word "serviceberry" for "sour cherry," and she has sold it commercially. The color is a rich dark purple and has the consistency of any other jelly. The taste to us was like apple jelly, but milder and blander. For this reason some recipes for serviceberry jellies and jams suggest adding the juice of something more tart, like chokecherries, apples, plums, or lemons.

Douglass gave us a recipe for steamed pudding. For each individual serving use ¼ cup fresh serviceberries, ¼ cup sliced peaches and 2 teaspoons sugar. Mix and place in the bottom of a large custard cup. Then make a dough, using 1 tablespoon biscuit mix (Bisquick), 1 tablespoon sugar and 1 tablespoon milk. Mix this together and drop on top of fruit mixture. Cover and put in steamer for 50 to 60 minutes.

Many similar recipes are in print using various fruits for which this fruit can be substituted. It seems a shame that this plant isn't used more, in view of its historical importance to the Indians and to early white settlers. Apparently the Ute Indians preferred to use the fruit of some serviceberries before it turned red or purple. In any event, this fruit would be an excellent emergency food either raw or cooked, and would be available over a period of several months.

Species:

One to six species have been recorded for the West by different workers who couldn't quite agree. However, the one illustrated (*A. alnifolia*), seems to be very widely distributed. Two other species closely resemble it (*A. utahensis* and *A. pumila*), these with smaller fruits.

Opuntia spp.
PRICKLYPEAR, TUNA, INDIAN FIG

Description:

Plants small to rather tall and tree-shaped; stems in joints or segments, these commonly flattened as in the illustration called "prickly pears" but in some species, roundish in cross-section (these often called "candelabra cacti" or "cholla"), these stem segments bearing patches of spines, these spines of two general kinds borne together; large ones that are stiff and sharp like a needle (but not hooked), and numerous minute ones (glochids) hardly big enough to see without a lens; leaves very small but fleshy, borne with the spine clusters and soon falling, leaving only a scar behind; flowers relatively large and showy, usually pink, purple, rose, reddish, yellow or greenish-yellow in color; petals and stamens many (11 or more) to a flower; fruit dry or fleshy, borne below the flower parts (inferior) instead of within or above it, bearing spines or glochids; seeds flattened.

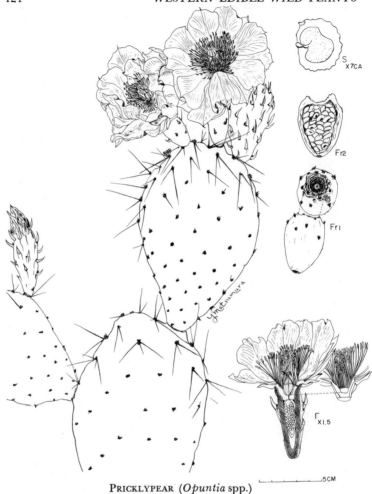

PRICKLYPEAR (*Opuntia* spp.)

Dry slopes and deserts. Scattered over all the West especially in the southern and drier parts of the area.

The following discussion mostly has to do with the kinds having flattened stem segments and bearing fleshy fruits at maturity.

Use:

The prickly pear cacti are plants of many uses, especially the ones with very pulpy fruits which are very important in Mexico. There they are sold in the markets as "tuna" secured from plants that may have been cultivated. Some of our wild species have fruits that have a much thinner layer of pulp between the rind and the seeds, but they are still edible, although they do vary considerably in palatability. As far as we know no cactus is poisonous. In fact, many kinds have been used as emergency cattle feed, after the spines are burned off with a blow torch. Spineless varieties of prickly pear have been developed for possible cultivation.

The large spines are a painful nuisance of course, but, except in rare instances, are not dangerous. The minute, barbed, bristle-like spines (glochids) are the ones to be feared. They may penetrate and work into the flesh, causing trouble for days afterwards. We once saw a public speaker holding a prickly pear in his bare hands in order to demonstrate his message more effectively. Out of curiosity we made a point of observing him the next day and found, as we expected, that both of his hands were red and swollen. Colyer found these bristles in ninety percent of the feces examined in studying the ancient Indian Ruins at Mesa Verde National Park. She then courageously tried eating some of the fresh fruits with the bristles intact and strangely enough, beyond a pricking of the tongue, the bristles produced no ill effect. The Indians are said to have rubbed off the spines but we were never able to get rid of the bristles either in that fashion or by burning them off. Anyone who has viewed these sharp-pointed little needles under a strong lens, with their lateral rows of barbs standing out like the ones on a fishhook, will surely use extreme caution in handling any part of the plant afterwards. Try burning them off if you wish, rubbing them off with leather gloves or scraping them off with a knife. In any case be respectful of them, even though you may not be able to see them.

The fruit can be split down one side, opened up, and the central seeds removed. The pulp layer can then be scraped away and eaten raw if you wish. You should find it sweet and gelatinous; at least the native kinds we have tried were very pleasant. The pulp is used in various ways as one would any fleshy fruit. Here is a recipe for cactus jelly we liked.

Prickly Pear Jelly

Wash and scald fruits. Remove spots but not prickles. Cut in halves and cook 15 minutes barely covered with water. Pour in bag and squeeze out the juice.

3 cups cactus juice	½ cup lemon juice
1 package powdered pectin	4½ cups sugar
(such as Sure-Jell)	

Mix juices and pectin. Place over high heat and stir until the mixture comes to a full rolling boil. Add sugar. Boil hard 1½ minutes stirring constantly. Remove from heat, skim, pour into scalded glasses and seal immediately with paraffin.

The Indians often dried the pulp in the sun. We tried this and after an interval of years we found it still in good condition. It may be used in any of the ways that dried fruit of any kind can be prepared for the table.

The seeds can be dried and stored for future use. The Indians parched them, ground them to a meal and used this in gruel or cakes. The young stem segments can be peeled and the contents eaten raw. We found them watery and mucilaginous, so much so that it was actually difficult to chew the pieces. This combined with a rather sour taste made us conclude that it would be much better to eat them only in cases of extreme need. The segments can be roasted or boiled, and the peel separated. Then the contents can be further prepared in various ways. One of us ate them sliced and mixed with scrambled eggs, pronouncing them "pleasant tasting."

The cacti can be life savers in the desert, providing both liquid and food in emergencies. The use of the barrel cacti in providing water is well known and has undoubtedly saved many lives.

Species:

We have over 30 species of *Opuntia* in our area, the most of them confined to the southern deserts with only a few of general distribution. Only about 7 bear fleshy edible fruit. However, several cacti in other genera (like the giant saguaro) have valuable fruits. We know of no poisonous cacti—painful ones, yes!

Helianthus spp.
SUNFLOWER

Description:

Annual or perennial plants, sometimes bearing tubers; stems branched or unbranched, often tall and thick for non-woody plants; leaves from narrow to broadly heart-shaped; individual flowers of 2 kinds clustered together in the same terminal head, the marginal strap-shaped ones usually yellow, the central tubular ones yellow or tinged with reddish-purple or brownish-red. The annual species with large seeds (achenes) are the ones most used. The common cultivated sunflower, with the taller thicker stem bearing a single large head, has been developed from one of these and has been called by botanists *H. annuus* variety *macrocarpus.*

Plains, prairies and valleys, and often on disturbed and dry ground. Sunflowers are distributed over all the West, often abundant enough to paint whole fields yellow.

SUNFLOWER (*Helianthus annuus*)

Use:

    The seeds (achenes) of the cultivated variety are now sold in almost every grocery store, but of course are larger than those of the wild type. The sunflower has always been a favorite food source of the Indians, probably from prehistoric times, and was apparently cultivated by some of the tribes.

The seeds were gathered by the Indians, parched and sometimes eaten whole. This we have tried and found the thin hulls could be readily eaten along with the kernel. Of course, the seeds can be ground and the hulls removed. Gibbons suggested an interesting method. If you have a food grinder available run the seed through a plate just large enough to crack the hulls. Dump the mixture in a bowl of water and the hulls will float to the top where they can be skimmed off. Then drain off the water and dry the kernels, using heat if necessary. Perhaps the hulls can be winnowed out in a breeze, or will come to the top on shaking the mixture. The kernels can be ground and the meal or flour used alone, or it can be mixed with cornmeal to make soup, mush, gruel or bread.

According to one report, the entire "seeds" can be roasted and ground as a substitute for coffee. Also, the ground seeds can be boiled until the oil, which is said to be about 20% of the contents, rises to the surface. This can be skimmed off and used as a cooking oil. The Hopi Indians still use this oil for greasing a hot flat rock on which they cook their blue cornmeal paper bread. The sunflower seeds appear to be worth trying under any condition, but appear to be particularly valuable as an emergency food. They occur in great abundance; we have all seen entire fields showing an almost solid sheet of yellow from the heads. The yellow marginal flowers are sometimes chewed as emergency food by Boy Scouts. In addition to the above mentioned uses of the plant, the young heads are reported to be edible when boiled in water and eaten like Brussels sprouts. This would be worth trying, but the plant contains a sticky, unpleasant smelling resin that we suspect may affect the taste. Perhaps the water will remove it.

Apparently the seeds of all the species of sunflower are edible. There are a few perennial ones that produce thickenings on the roots that resemble tubers. The most famous one is *Helianthus tuberosus,* usually called "Jerusalem artichoke." These tubers were extensively used by the Indians who boiled, baked or fried them like potatoes. The early pioneers learned their value and they were taken back to the Old World where they were cultivated. These tubers are reported to sometimes grow to be over two inches in diameter, and are said to be nutritious and flavorful. They seem to lack starch and therefore may be eaten by persons who are suffering from ailments precluding that substance in their diet. The tubers are said to contain a mucilaginous substance that may remain in the water after boiling, and can be used to thicken soup. Jerusalem artichoke seems to be rather uncommon in our area.

Species:

About 10 species of *Helianthus* are recorded for the West. The common widely distributed, annual, large-seeded ones are *H. annuus* and *H. petiolaris.*

Oryzopsis spp.
RICEGRASS

Description:

Perennial bunchgrasses; stems usually erect or nearly so, hollow in the center; leaves long and narrow (grasslike); seed-bearing units (spikelets) large for grasses in general, up to ½ inch long exclusive of a slender terminal awn that breaks off readily.

Plains, valleys, woods and slopes. Widespread throughout the West, usually at low to medium elevations.

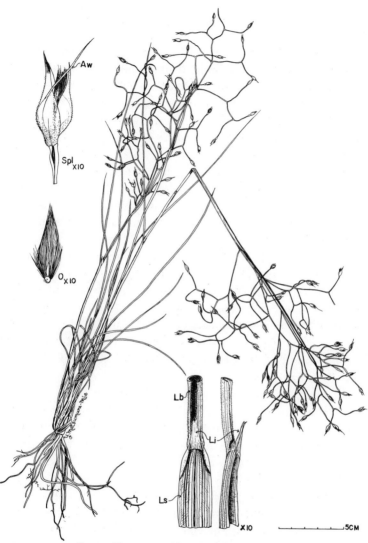

INDIAN RICEGRASS (*Oryzopsis hymenoides*)

Use:

    The seeds of these plants are rather large when compared with those of native grasses in general. For that reason they have been used as food by the Indians since prehistoric times, and were often important in their economy as the common name suggests. The so-called "seed" is rather plump and invested with two close-fitting outer scales, these are often covered with fine white hairs as in the Indian ricegrass as illustrated. The Indians got rid of these hairs by holding a bunch of the stems with the heads extending close to a fire. Apparently the hairs were burned off, and the seeds dropped into a pan or rock below. These seeds can also be gathered in a pan and several small live coals placed in among them. By shaking the mixture, the seeds will not only have any hairs burned off but they will be parched at the same time.

In any event, they were often ground to form a meal that was used in various ways, as a mush or gruel, to thicken soup or to make cakes. The seeds of one of these were found by several workers to be about 18-20% starch in one sample, with about 6% of sugars. Compared with our cultivated grains this is not a very high percentage of food, but the plants are reported to have a pleasing taste and would certainly make an excellent emergency food.

It might be advisable to try winnowing out the ground-up chaff from the meal, but we think this would not be necessary, in any case it sounds rather impractical. One thing is certain, they are often available in quantities in just the areas where they might be desperately needed as survival food.

As far as we know, any grass will produce edible seeds, providing it is not affected by a fungus infection such as ergot. The ergot forms a black, cylindrical or cigar-shaped body that replaces the grass seed but may be larger. This mass is poisonous, but fortunately it is rather conspicuous. In an emergency we would not hesitate to select any grass that is abundant in the area, and has reasonably large seeds. These we would parch and try to eat them whole, or attempt to grind them into a meal or flour between rocks.

Species:

Orysopsis asperifolia (mountain ricegrass) is an eastern species coming into the eastern part of our area. It has a seed about twice as long as common ricegrass, with fewer, shorter hairs covering it. It has been reported to be very good as a food source and should be equal or superior to our more common ones. However, we have never found it in any abundance in our area.

Our common and most widely distributed one is Indian ricegrass (the species illustrated) noted for its peculiar branching of the inflorescence. However, about 5 others have been listed for our area.

Ephedra spp.

JOINTFIR, DESERT TEA, MEXICAN TEA, MORMON TEA, BRIGHAM YOUNG TEA, JOINTPINE

Description:

Branching shrubs usually 8 inches to 4 feet tall; twigs green to yellow-green in color, jointed-looking, rather rigid and wiry; leaves 2 or 3 in each circle of the stem, very small and inconspicuous, in fact reduced to teeth; flowers small, not colorful or conspicuous; seeds up to $\frac{1}{2}$ inch long.

Sandy or rocky plains, slopes and deserts. Scattered over the West, particularly in the dry southern part of the area.

Use:

As the common names suggest, these plants have been extensively used by both the Indians and white people for making a tea. Sometimes it was taken as a tonic for its reputed medicinal effects, but many persons used it rather regularly by preference as a beverage. The greenish twigs were gathered,

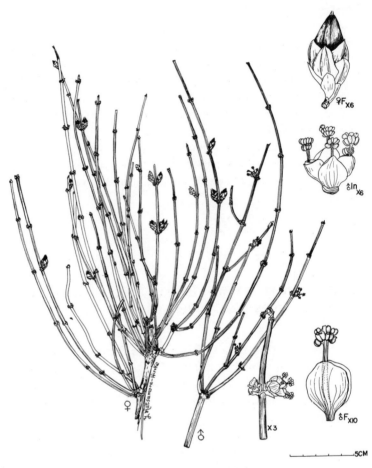

JOINTFIR (*Ephedra viridis*)

and were either used fresh or allowed to dry for later use. We
have tried them both ways and can see little difference in the
flavor. These twigs were boiled in water for just a few minutes,
and the mixture allowed to steep for 5 to 15 minutes. The
liquid took on a yellowish or pinkish color, and had a very ac-

ceptable odor and taste. You should experiment with varying amounts to suit your taste, but we suggest you start by using a small cup of broken stems to 6 or 8 cups of water. The taste may take a bit of getting used to, and we have never learned to like it quite as well as we do commercial tea. But it certainly does make a very acceptable substitute. The Indians often roasted the twigs before using them, and claimed this improved the flavor. The plants seem to contain certain alkaloids such as pseudoephedrin and tannin, but apparently our species does not produce the well-known drug "ephedrin," as does the related *E. sinica* of China. Many people have written to us inquiring about this matter, sometimes they are interested in the possibility of harvesting the plant commercially for the drug, or often they are wondering if prolonged use of the tea might have harmful effects. We know of no immediate or cumulative ill effects from using the tea, but this does not mean it could not occasionally happen.

The Indians roasted the seeds of jointfir and ate them whole, or ground them into a meal or flour. The bread made from this product is said to be bitter tasting. These plants are often abundant in the desert area, just where an emergency food and a stimulating beverage might be desperately needed.

Species:

The one illustrated (*E. viridis*) is widely distributed and the one we have tried the most. However, about 6 more are recorded from our area. Of these *E. torreyana, E. nevadensis* and *E. californica* are reported to make acceptable tea. We would not hesitate to try any of the species ourselves.

CHAPTER IV: POISONOUS PLANTS
(like Poison Ivy and Death Camas)

EVER SINCE PRIMITIVE MAN first tried eating the plants growing about him, he has been confronted with the bitter realization that while most of them are harmless, many of them are poisonous to some degree, and cause him discomfort, sickness, or even death. We like to think that nature is kind and benevolent, and usually it is. However, we know that sometimes it can be exceedingly cruel. In every pond, in every river, in every woodland, and on every mountain or prairie, there waits for us pillage, starvation, and death. There is a sad reality. As far as eating native plants is concerned, all nature asks of us, in order to escape her ill effects, is a certain amount of "knowledge." If you know the common poisonous species as you would recognize an acquaintance on the street, then you are as safe eating these native plants as if you were dining at home or in a modern restaurant. This chapter discusses and illustrates only the very common most harmful ones of this area. Many states put out illustrated bulletins on additional species toxic to livestock. The most complete and up-to-date general treatment on this particular subject is the one by Kingsbury (*Poisonous Plants of the United States and Canada,* 1964). A few general observations on poisonous plants are given below in the hope that they may prove to be of value to you:

1. There is no general test for poisonous plants, such as the presence or absence of milky juice. Many plants with this milky juice are edible (see *Taraxacum,* the dandelion), and some of the most poisonous species lack it altogether.

2. The fact that wild animals eat the plant is no guarantee that it will not be poisonous to you. For example, just because birds often eat the berries and seeds of poison ivy is no indication that you can do the same with impunity.

3. Livestock usually do avoid poisonous plants if any others are available. However, when they are hungry for green foliage, as when they have been confined for several days, or in the spring of the year, they often graze on poisonous plants they would ordinarily avoid.

4. Some plants produce their poisonous substances when wilted, such as the twigs of chokecherries.

5. The poisonous property may be concentrated or even confined to one part of the plant body.

6. In some cases cooking seems to destroy the poisonous substances, in whole or in part, but this is not a general rule.

7. Do not use any wild plant resembling parsley or wild carrot unless you are absolutely sure of your species.

8. Do not use white- or red-colored berries without being absolutely sure of the plant.

9. Eat blue or black berries but with caution; even here it is best to know the species tried.

10. Better avoid all fungi (mushrooms and toadstools) unless you know them to be safe.

11. Do not eat any plant from soils known to contain selenium, or that support plants known to be "indicators" of selenium.

12. Be sure you know the plant in its very young stages, if this is the time it is to be used.

13. Never suppose a plant to be edible just because it bears some resemblance to a well-known species, such as to the fruits or roots at the grocery store.

14. Always be cautious in trying out a new plant even though you are absolutely sure of its identity. Remember that the poisonous effects can be cumulative.

15. Read over the tests for edibility as given in the Introduction. *The best advice is to know and avoid the common poisonous plants of your locality.*

The authors have been mildly criticized by a few persons for including an unpleasant chapter such as this, especially for mentioning the effects of some poisonous plants on livestock. Now we do not claim close kinship to a horse or cow but we doubt if we would enjoy eating a plant that had caused even a slight illness to one of them!

Ignoring an evil certainly does not minimize its effects. Although we advise treating poisonous plants with the respect they deserve, we do not suggest that fear of them should prevent you from using any wild plant as food. With proper and reasonable precautions on your part they will not harm you. Where poisonous plants are concerned though, being reasonably certain isn't enough: be positive!

Cicuta douglasii (*C. occidentalis*)
Water Hemlock, Poison Water Hemlock

Description:
Perennial plants from thick rootstocks that develop crosspartitions in older plants at about ground level (see illustration); stems 2 to 4 feet tall; leaflets 1 to 4 inches long with the lateral veins ending in the notches between the teeth (not in the tooth points as in some rather similar plants); petals white, small; fruits small, about $\frac{1}{8}$ inch long.

Grows in swamps, ditches, along streams, and in wet meadows from the Rocky Mountains west to the Pacific. Our plant looks a great deal like the one present in the eastern half of the United States. We seldom see it growing above 8,500 feet in our area.

WATER HEMLOCK (*Cicuta douglasii*)

Effects:

This species (with its eastern relative) has gained the reputation of being the most poisonous plant in the North Temperate Zone. The poison is concentrated mostly in the lower part of the stems or roots. It often causes death to livestock, and it is sometimes stated that a piece the size of a walnut will cause the death of a cow. Human beings have sometimes been poisoned by water hemlock, eating the underground parts, having mistaken them for various edible roots like parsnips. Children will sometimes do this, often with fatal results. It is said that a piece the size of a marble can cause death to a man.

The poison is very virulent and causes violent convulsions. Vomiting should be induced at once and a strong cathartic administered. Everyone should become familiar with this poisonous plant whether or not they intend to eat edible plants. It would be best to avoid anything that even looks like it, and eradicate it if it grows near your home.

Species:

C. douglasii (the one illustrated) is the common one of the West although a few others are present in the extreme western and northern parts. The one in the eastern United States, *C. maculata,* is similar to our common species in appearance and poisonous properties.

Conium maculatum
POISON HEMLOCK, EUROPEAN POISON HEMLOCK

Description:

Biennial plants from stout taproots, the lower part of the stem or crown with few or no cross-partitions separating cavities (as in *Cicuta*); stems 1½ to 10 feet tall, branching,

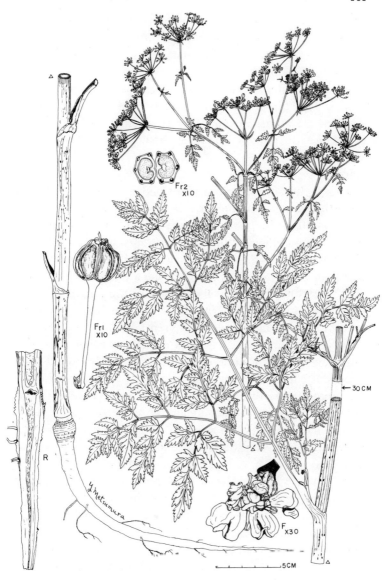

POISON HEMLOCK (*Conium maculatum*)

spotted with brown or reddish-brown dots; leaves filmy or fern-like, the whole compound leaf often as much as a foot long; flowers small, white in color; fruits seedlike, small, each about ⅛ inch long.

Introduced into North America from other continents and now widely distributed. We usually find it from low to medium elevations in our area. It is often found in waste places, usually in moist ground, in ditches or in valley bottoms.

Effects:

This is the famous poison plant said to have been used by the Athenians to kill Socrates. It may be more poisonous at some seasons of the year, and some parts of the plant seem to be worse than others. It has even been used as a food plant in the early spring! We recommend avoiding it and also any plant that in any way resembles it, unless you are absolutely familiar with everything involved. The action of the poison does not cause convulsions as in *Cicuta* but has a numbing, paralyzing effect. Livestock sometimes have been poisoned by eating the fresh plant. Human beings have sometimes eaten the roots, mistaking them for those of parsnips or cow parsnips, with disastrous effects. The seed-like fruits have also been mistaken for anise, especially since the poison hemlock often grows around gardens, sometimes under the name of Queen Ann's Lace (a name also applied to wild carrot). The seeds, especially when partly developed, seem to be particularly poisonous and were said to have been used by Indians to poison their war arrows. Children have been poisoned by blowing on whistles made from the hollow stems, but judging from our own experience, this is probably not a very great hazard. We have often had the plant sent in with the story that children have used it for whistles, but so far we have no reports of any serious effect. Everyone should learn this plant and attempt to eradicate it in their immediate area.

Species:

No other species. However, many edible plants belong to the same family and have a superficial resemblance to this poisonous plant.

Zigadenus spp. *(Zygadenus)*
DEATH CAMAS, ZYGADENE

Description:

Plants perennial from bulbs; leaves narrow and grasslike, crowded near the base of the stems; flowers in rather short to elongated clusters, each flower with segments ⅛ to ⅜ inch long, greenish-white to yellowish-white in color; fruit a dry pod (capsule) with 3 inner compartments, these with several to many seeds.

Meadows, plains and open slopes. From Canada south to Florida, Texas, New Mexico, Arizona and California, therefore rather generally distributed throughout the West, from low elevations up to 12,000 feet in the mountains.

Effects:

All the different species of *Zigadenus* are poisonous to a greater or lesser degree and should be avoided by everyone. All parts of the plant are toxic, including the bulbs, leaves, flowers and seeds. The various kinds of death camas cause serious losses to livestock in our area, particularly affecting sheep. In a dry spring, the leaves of these plants may develop vigorously by obtaining moisture from the bulbs; often these green shoots are the only succulent growth in sight. The hungry animals will sometimes graze on the plants, especially if they have been penned up for a while, when under more normal conditions they might avoid them completely. Cattle

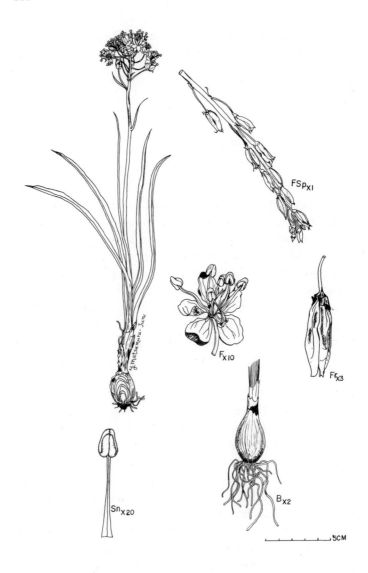

FSp_{X1}

F_{X10}

Fr_{X3}

Sn_{X20}

B_{X2}

5CM

DEATH CAMAS (*Zigadenus gramineus*)

and horses seem to be less affected, probably because of their grazing habits. Even chickens have been poisoned, but seldom hogs, since they have the habit of vomiting and thus getting rid of some of the poisonous material.

The bulbs are the most dangerous parts to human beings, since they may be easily gathered by mistake for those of the wild onion, mariposa (or sego) lily or camass. We have actually observed people in this locality indiscriminately gathering wild onion and death camas bulbs to be used as food! The Indians apparently had this same problem because it is reported that they sometimes gathered these bulbs, mistaking them for edible ones, with disastrous results. To make it worse, even the dried bulbs kept their toxic effect, so the danger to the Indians could extend well into the winter. Children at play have been poisoned by eating the bulbs.

Certainly anyone utilizing such thickened underground structures for food in this area should learn to recognize death camas and, in addition, learn to distinguish the plant from other bulb-bearing species that are edible (see *Allium* spp., *Camassia* spp. and *Calochortus* spp.).

The symptoms of poisoning by death camas are salivation, weakness, finally lowering of the body temperature, coma, and nausea with a tendency to vomit. If you suspect that this plant has been eaten by someone, then by all means encourage free vomiting and get the sick person to a doctor as soon as possible. If this cannot be done, we can only recommend keeping the victim as quiet as possible and administering orally a water solution of common baking soda. This could certainly do no great harm and would be worth trying in cases where human beings have been poisoned by death camas.

There may be several poisonous substances present, but the primary one seems to be an alkaloid called "Zygadenine." It is claimed that the toxic effect may be twice as potent as that from strychnine.

Species:

The poisonous effects seem to vary among the different species. For example, *Z. elegans* seems to be less dangerous than *Z. gramineus* (the one illustrated). About 8 species are recorded for the West but the most of them resemble the drawing very closely.

Rhus radicans (*R. rydbergii, R. toxicodendron, Toxico-dendron rydbergii*)
POISON IVY, POISON OAK

Description:

Shrubs or vinelike plants, often with aerial rootlets; leaves with 3 divisions (leaflets), the stalk to the middle division longer than those on the lateral ones (see illustration); leaflets about 1½ to 8 inches long; flowers small, the petals about ⅛ inch long, yellowish-white in color; fruit rather dry but berry-like, globe-shaped, about ¼ inch wide, yellowish-white in color.

Hillsides, plains and woods. The various varieties are found throughout North America. Widespread in the West, often found in valleys along streams, especially near picnic areas!

Effects:

The western form of the species is usually a rather low non-climbing or a low-climbing shrub. Poison ivy contains a non-volatile oil in all, or in practically all, of its parts; an oil which is poisonous to most people when it comes in contact with the skin. Some believe that about 2 or 3 out of 4 people are sensitive to it in varying degrees. The self-styled "immune" people may be surprised some day to find themselves down with a severe attack of poison ivy. Apparently the degree of contact, the growth stage of the plant, even the toxicity of the

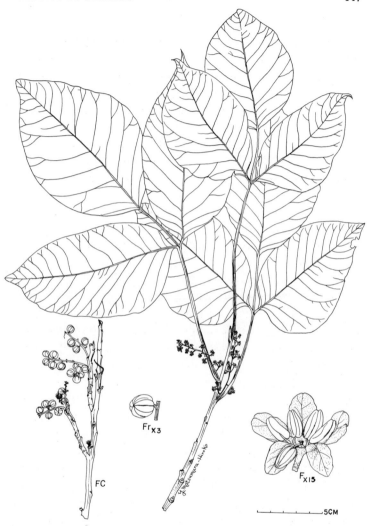

POISON IVY (*Rhus radicans*)

individual ivy plant you chance to meet, possibly your own
physical condition at the time, all affect the degree of re-

sistance. We once saw a youth, who handled poison ivy safely all summer, develop a severe case of poisoning in late summer. This plant should be recognized and avoided by everyone. This is difficult to do since inanimate objects such as tool handles, rope, shoes and clothing can be contaminated by the poison and cause trouble for many months afterwards. Some people swear they get attacks of the rash by merely being near the plant. This appears doubtful from experiments that have been made, although dust and smoke have been known to transport the oil through the atmosphere. Remember, the oil is nonvolatile and does not diffuse out through the air. The toxic substance has been called "urushoil" and causes the characteristic burning, rash, itching and blisters that almost everyone has experienced or observed in others. We have heard scores of remedies, preventives and cures for poison ivy. The commonest preventive suggestion is to wash the affected parts soon after exposure with a strong nonoily laundry soap. Preventive creams and injections have not had uniform success. In light cases, the following measures have been suggested: application of baking soda or Epsom salts, one or two teaspoonsful to a cup of water; a fluid extract of *Grindelia* diluted with about 8 parts of water; a 5 percent solution of potassium permanganate or wet compresses of boric acid solution. In moderate or severe cases, it is wise to consult a doctor, especially if the parts affected are near the eyes. Deaths have been reported in extreme cases of poison ivy poisoning.

Cases are on record where the leaves or the attractive looking whitish berries have been eaten, usually by children, with poisonous effect on the lining of the digestive tract. Birds eat the berries apparently without harm, and the plant is occasionally grazed by livestock or game animals without much effect. However, as indicated before, this is a good plant for all human beings to avoid.

Species:

Not all the species of *Rhus* cause this dermatitis. The far western *R. diversiloba* is toxic but usually differs from the widely distributed *R. radicans* by having the leaflets more or less lobed or cut. The poison sumac (*R. vernix*) of the eastern United States is poisonous to many people, but it has more than 3 parts or segments to a leaf, more like a sumac than an ivy.

Cannabis sativa
HEMP, MARIJUANA, INDIAN HEMP

Description:

Stems simple to branched, 3 to 8 feet tall; leaves compound in "finger-like" fashion as shown, the individual leaflets 2 to 6 inches long; flowers small and not at all colorful, the pollen-bearing flowers and seed-producing flowers on separate plants (staminate and pistillate plants).

Waste places, along ditches and roadsides or along fields possibly as an escape from cultivation. This plant is common east of our area, but we seldom see it growing in the West.

Effects:

The seeds of hemp can be used as food and are said to be nutritious and even stimulating. They have been parched and mixed into a batter and fried into cakes. This could be done with caution in an emergency. Kephart says that, in Belgium, the young shoots are used as a substitute for asparagus. However, the plant contains poisonous alkaloids and, as is well known, is smoked in various parts of the world for its narcotic effects.

At present there is a good deal of controversy as to its actual

MARIJUANA (*Cannabis sativa*)

harmful effects, especially the consequences of prolonged use. From our standpoint it is considered a poisonous plant and it would seem better to avoid using it as food at all.

Species:

Only the one listed above. It has been cultivatcd at one time as a source of fiber in the eastern and middle United States.

Amanita spp.
AMANITA, FLY AGARIC, DEATHCUP, DEATH ANGEL

Description:

These fungi produce the familiar mushroom or toadstool-like structure, consisting of a central stalk and an umbrella-like terminal portion bearing radiating gills below, these bearing the small reproductive spores. The stalk arises from a basal cup (the volva) and bears a veil (annulus) toward the top of the stem, marking the place where the once curled-in edges of the cup broke away as it opened out. The color is pure white or pale yellow (as in *A. phalloides*) or the top may be yellow to brown varying to red with the surface often flecked with white scales or spots (as in *A. muscaria*). The radiating gills are white and are free from the upper part of the stalk.

The two described above are rather widespread in the West, especially *A. muscaria* (Fly Agaric, the one illustrated). Fortunately, the more deadly *A. phalloides* (Death Angel) gets scarcer westward and seems to be absent from the Pacific States. However, other poisonous species may take its place (like *A. pantherina* with brownish caps).

Because of their relatively low food value and the poisonous properties of a few, we do not recommend eating fungi at all, either in an emergency or as a casual hobby (see next page).

└———————┘5CM

AMANITA (*Amanita muscaria*)

Effects:

These fungi usually grow in wooded, shaded areas but may appear at the edges of clearings and might be mistaken by the novice for several commonly used edible species. It is stated that one or two of these "umbrellas" can cause death, even if mixed with harmless fungi.

The hobby of gathering fungi for food is both dangerous and interesting. The suggestions we would make would be:

1. Learn the poisonous species, not only by their general

appearance but by their actual diagnostic characters. For example, any species of *Amanita* has the following characters:

    a. Presence of a basal cup (volva).

    b. Presence of a veil (annulus) on the stem.

    c. White colored gills and spores.

    d. Gills free from the upper part of the stem.

There are other poisonous kinds of fungi but the Amanitas are the worst. If you avoid all fungi with the above four characteristics, there is a reasonably good chance you won't die from eating fungi!

2. Learn edible species one by one, by general appearance and by their diagnostic characters. Stick to these and if you must experiment with a new one, try only a very small piece at first, then a larger one after an interval of an hour or two, etc. Unless you are willing to do all this, you had better leave the fungi alone.

Species:

Unfortunately, the species of *Amanita* are difficult to arrange properly taxonomically, but about 25 have been recorded for the United States. Only a few of these are in our area. Some of them are actually considered to be edible. Much depends on how confident one is of one's ability to identify the species correctly!

Index to Scientific Names

Index to Common Names